The Usborne Book of World
GEOGRAPHY
With World Atlas

Contents

Written and compiled by Jenny Tyler, Lisa Watts, Carol Bowyer, Roma Trundle and Annabel Warrender.

Consultant editors: Dr Martin Angel, Iain Bain, Pamela Bowen, Barry Dufour, Dr Peter Loizos and Ray Pask.

Illustrated by Bob Hersey, Rob McCaig, Joseph McEwan and Graham Round. Map artwork by Product Support Graphics, Ltd, Derby.

Designed by Graham Round, Bob Scott and Anna Barnard.

Part One

The Earth We Live On

What you will find in this part of the book.

The Story of the Earth

The Earth is about 4,600 million years old. It is hard to imagine such a long time. To help you we have used a huge sand glass.

It takes 4,700 million years for the sand to run through it. Watch the sand glass to see how old the Earth is at each stage in the story.

6 Skeletons give us a good idea of what the first animals looked like. Dinosaurs were a group of animals which lived about 160 million years ago.

4,700 million years ago

1

Scientists think the Earth probably began as a great, swirling cloud of dust and gases. This cloud grew very hot and changed into a ball of liquid rock.

4,600 million years ago

2

The ball of rock slowly cooled and a thin crust of rock hardened on the outside. Hot, liquid rock from inside broke through the crust in lots of places.

Tree ferns like these still grow in hot, wet places today.

The Stegosaurus had three brains, though none of them were very big. It had one brain in its head, one in its tail and one in its back.

One of the first flying animals was called the Rhamphorhynchus. It was hairy and had sharp teeth in its beak.

The huge Brontosaurus only ate plants. From its nose to its tail it was about 22 metres.

3,800 million years ago

Enormous clouds of steam and gases collected round the Earth. There were violent storms and rain poured down from the clouds. Floods made the first seas.

2,500 million years ago

Plants began to grow in the seas, though there were no animals yet. Animals cannot live without oxygen gas to breathe and at first there was no oxygen.

570–400 million years ago

As plants grow they make oxygen which animals can breathe. The first animals lived in the sea. Then bigger animals developed and they crawled out on to the land.

This picture shows some of the first people on Earth. They lived in caves and made tools out of stone.

There have been people on the Earth for the last million years. This seems a very long time, but look at the sand glass. The last grains of sand have nearly fallen through and people have only just appeared in the story. The Earth existed for about 4,599 million years without any people.

The Iguanodon walked upright and could run faster than other dinosaurs. It had spikes like daggers on its thumbs.

Inside the Earth

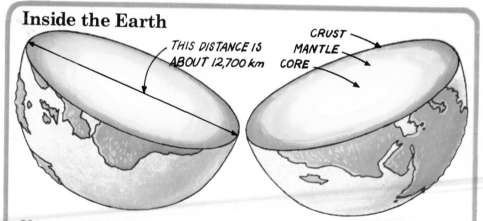

THIS DISTANCE IS ABOUT 12,700 km

CRUST
MANTLE
CORE

If you could cut the Earth in half, it would look something like this.

The *crust* is a thin layer of rock between 8 and 64 kilometres thick.

Beneath the crust, the rock is hot and toffee-like. This part is called the *mantle*. The rock in the mantle is called *magma*.

The centre of the Earth is called the *core*. It is too deep inside the Earth for scientists to examine. But they think it is probably made of very hot, liquid metal.

How the World is Changing Shape

How the land moves

Scientists think that the land is moving very slowly. Find out how this is happening by following the numbers round this picture.

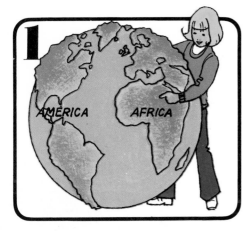

1 Look at the shapes of Africa and America. The two bits of land look as though they could fit together like jigsaw pieces. Perhaps they were once joined up.

2 There are dinosaur bones in Africa and in America. The huge animals could not have swum across the sea. But if the land was joined they could have walked across.

1 The Earth's crust is made of pieces which fit very closely together. Each piece is called a *plate*. Here, we have lifted one of the plates up for you to see.

9 Most of the world's volcanoes and earthquakes happen at the edge of plates because they are weak spots in the Earth's crust.

8 Some plates are moving towards each other. The edge of one plate rides up over the other one. The plate underneath melts as it sinks down into the mantle.

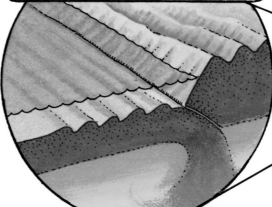

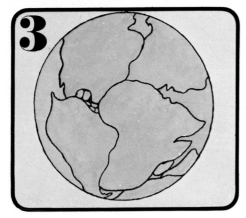

3 Scientists think the land was once joined up like this. It made one big land called Pangaea. About 190 million years ago, Pangaea began to split up.

4 The land is still moving. Telephone cables under the Atlantic Ocean have snapped because America is moving 25 millimetres away from Europe every year.

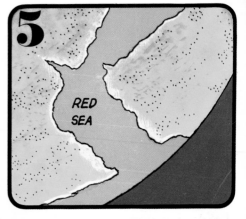

5 This is what the Red Sea looks like from a space ship. The land seems to have been torn apart. The land is still moving and the Red Sea is getting wider every year.

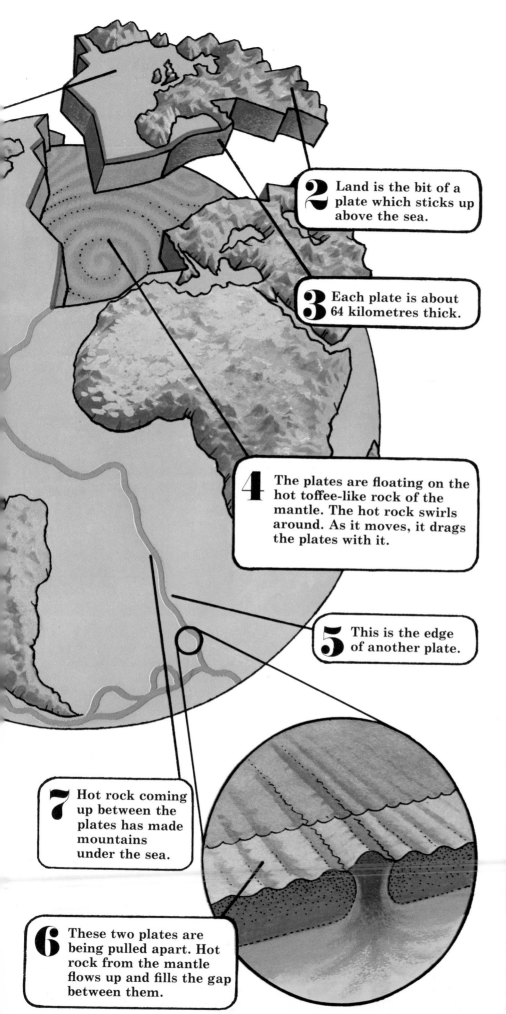

2 Land is the bit of a plate which sticks up above the sea.

3 Each plate is about 64 kilometres thick.

4 The plates are floating on the hot toffee-like rock of the mantle. The hot rock swirls around. As it moves, it drags the plates with it.

5 This is the edge of another plate.

7 Hot rock coming up between the plates has made mountains under the sea.

6 These two plates are being pulled apart. Hot rock from the mantle flows up and fills the gap between them.

Building mountains

The remains of sea creatures have been found in rocks in the Himalayan mountains. Tremendous forces must have pushed these rocks up from under the sea.

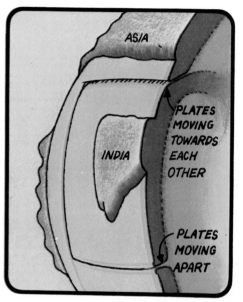

ASIA

PLATES MOVING TOWARDS EACH OTHER

INDIA

PLATES MOVING APART

There used to be sea where the Himalayan mountains are. This was about 150 million years ago when India was being carried on its plate towards Asia.

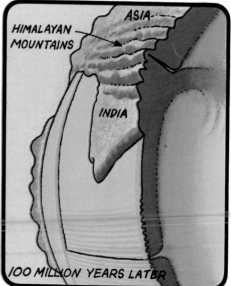

HIMALAYAN MOUNTAINS

ASIA

INDIA

100 MILLION YEARS LATER

Eventually, India bumped into Asia. The rocks under the sea between them were squeezed up to make gigantic mountains. These are the Himalayan mountains.

Rocks and Fossils

As soon as the Earth's rocky crust hardened, it began to wear away. Rain and wind attacked the rock and slowly broke it into bits of sand and mud. Rock is being worn away like this all the time. Over millions of years, high mountains become low hills.

The world would be a very flat place by now if no new rocks were being made. Some new rocks are made from bits of old rock. Others are made from the liquid rock inside the Earth.

Rain, wind and ice are wearing away the rocks. This is called *weathering*. Little bits of rock break off high mountains and make them sharp and jagged.

Rain washes the bits of rock into streams. They tumble and knock against each other in the water. This grinds them down into sand and mud and little stones.

Streams and rivers carry the sand and mud all the way to the sea. Thick layers of it slowly build up on the sea floor, along with bones and shells of sea creatures.

The muddy sand is packed down by the weight of more layers piling on top. It is pressed so hard that it becomes solid rock. Rock made like this is called *sedimentary rock.*

Some of the sedimentary rock made under the sea becomes dry land. Movements in the Earth's crust lift and bend the layers of rock and make it into new hills.

Rocks from inside the Earth

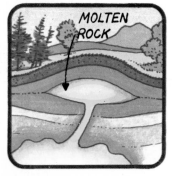

MOLTEN ROCK

MANY YEARS LATER ROCKS ABOVE ARE WORN AWAY

GRANITE

SLATE

Sometimes liquid rock from inside the Earth pushes its way into the crust. It may even break right through the crust and make a volcano. When this rock cools, it hardens and is called *igneous rock.*

A common igneous rock is granite.
Molten rock in the crust heats the rocks around it and changes them. They are then called *metamorphic rocks.* Slate is one of these.

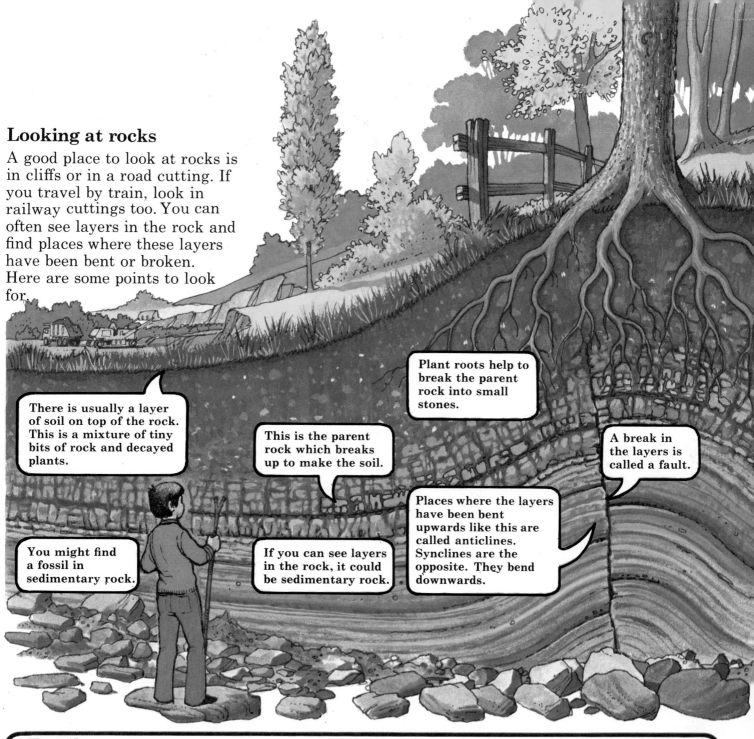

Looking at rocks

A good place to look at rocks is in cliffs or in a road cutting. If you travel by train, look in railway cuttings too. You can often see layers in the rock and find places where these layers have been bent or broken. Here are some points to look for.

There is usually a layer of soil on top of the rock. This is a mixture of tiny bits of rock and decayed plants.

Plant roots help to break the parent rock into small stones.

This is the parent rock which breaks up to make the soil.

A break in the layers is called a fault.

You might find a fossil in sedimentary rock.

If you can see layers in the rock, it could be sedimentary rock.

Places where the layers have been bent upwards like this are called anticlines. Synclines are the opposite. They bend downwards.

Fossils

FOSSIL OF AMMONITE

FOSSIL OF DINOSAUR BONES

Shapes of animals and plants which lived millions of years ago are sometimes found in sedimentary rocks. These are *fossils*. This is the fossil of an ammonite, a sea creature which lived at the same time as dinosaurs.

When the ammonite died, its shell was covered with sand and mud. This was all pressed down and the rock that formed had a pattern, or fossil, of the shell in it. Fossils tell us a lot about plants and animals that lived long ago.

The Earth in Space

Your address in space

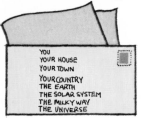

It is difficult to imagine how big space is. Our Earth is just one of millions of objects floating around in it. Most of these objects are *stars* —balls of hot gas which give out heat and light. Some are so far away that it would take millions of years to reach them.

These pictures show where you fit in the universe. Imagine you are writing your address in space. This is you in your house and your house in your street.

Your house is a small part of a town, so you write the name of your town next.

Your country is just a little bit of the land on the Earth. Land covers less than one-third of the Earth's surface. The rest is covered by sea.

The Earth is one of nine *planets* going round a star which we call the Sun. Together they are known as the *solar system*. Planets do not give out light like stars.

The solar system belongs to a group of 100,000 million stars called the Milky Way. This is our *galaxy*. On a clear night you can see it as a hazy glow in the sky.

The Moon

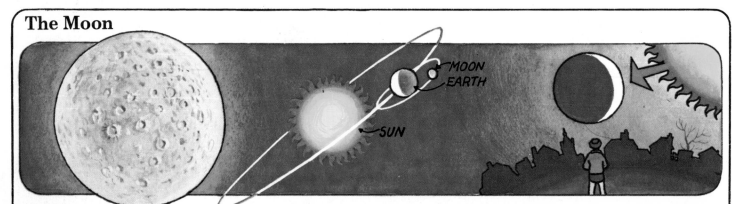

You can only see one side of the moon from Earth. Astronauts have seen the other side. The dents on the surface are craters.

The Moon takes about a month to go round the Earth. Other planets have moons too. Saturn has 10 and Jupiter has 13.

The Moon does not shine with light of its own. We see it because the Sun shines on it. Often part of it is in shadow.

This is your town in your country. Your town probably seems quite large. When you see it surrounded by other towns and countryside, it does not seem so big.

There are millions of galaxies in the universe. They are not all the same size or shape as our own. Some may contain planets like ours, but we do not know.

The planets

Pluto. Dark and cold.
Neptune. Giant, greeny-blue planet.

Uranus. Rings discovered in 1977.

Saturn. Big rings, probably made of dust and ice.

Jupiter. Largest planet in solar system.
Mars. Called the Red Planet as it is made of red rock.
Earth. Has one moon.
Venus. The hottest planet.
Mercury. Next to Sun.

Day and night

The Earth is spinning round all the time, though you cannot feel it. It takes 24 hours to spin round once.

Think of one place and follow it as the Earth goes round. For about 12 hours it is in light from the Sun. This is its day. Then it moves into the shadow behind the Earth and it is night for 12 hours.

MIDDAY

EARLY MORNING

SUNSET

SUNRISE

EARLY EVENING

MIDNIGHT

Summer and Winter

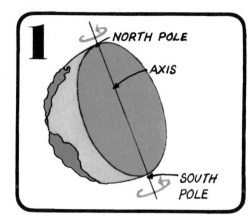

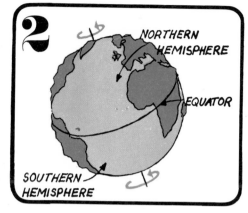

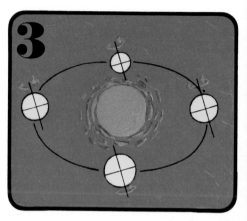

Before we can explain the seasons properly, we need to tell you some words to do with the Earth. First, there is the *axis*. This is the line through the middle of the Earth.

The *equator* is a line round the widest part of the Earth. The top half of the Earth is the *northern hemisphere* and the bottom half is the *southern hemisphere*.

The seasons change because the Earth's axis leans over to one side. On the Earth's trip round the Sun, first one hemisphere and then the other is closer to the Sun.

How the seasons change

Summer happens in the hemisphere that is closer to the Sun. It is winter in the other hemisphere. Follow the Earth round the Sun and see how the seasons change.

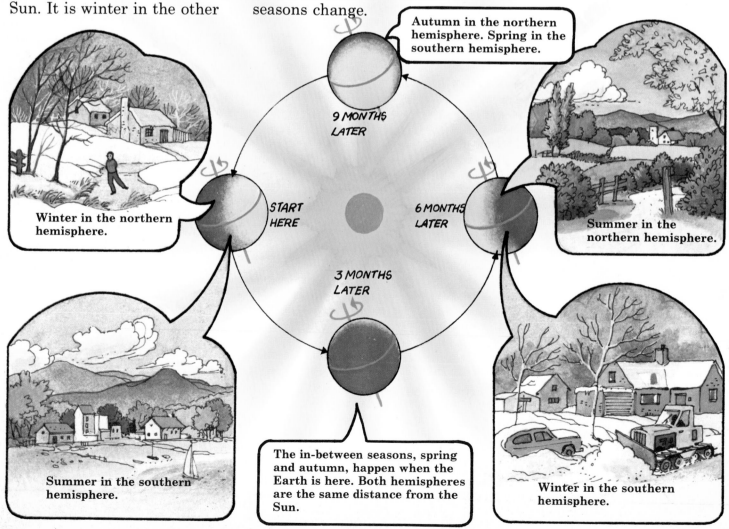

Autumn in the northern hemisphere. Spring in the southern hemisphere.

9 MONTHS LATER

6 MONTHS LATER

START HERE

3 MONTHS LATER

Winter in the northern hemisphere.

Summer in the northern hemisphere.

Summer in the southern hemisphere.

The in-between seasons, spring and autumn, happen when the Earth is here. Both hemispheres are the same distance from the Sun.

Winter in the southern hemisphere.

The Sky

The Earth is wrapped in a blanket of air called the *atmosphere*. This gets thinner and thinner as you move away from the Earth. There is no air at all beyond about 550 km, which is where the atmosphere ends and space begins.

The air is a mixture of gases. One of them is oxygen which we must breathe to stay alive. Another is carbon dioxide which plants need. There is also water in the air.

Most of our weather is made in the bottom 15 km of the atmosphere, so this is the bit we have shown here.

The highest clouds you can see are cirrus clouds. The air is very cold at this height and these clouds are made of little bits of ice.

There is very little air at the height at which jet planes fly. Air is pumped into the cabin for the passengers to breathe.

The air at this height is colder than the air at sea level, so high mountains are always covered with snow.

When there is a lot of water in the air, you can see it as clouds.

Mountaineers carry oxygen in tanks on their backs when they climb very high. This is because there is not enough oxygen in the air for them to breathe.

There is more water in the air near the Earth, so the clouds there are bigger than those higher up.

Wind is just the air moving around.

Carbon dioxide is the gas in the air that plants need so that they can grow.

The air is like a blanket round the Earth. It keeps it warm at night. During the day, it protects us from the Sun's rays. We would be burnt to cinders if it were not there.

The air is heavy. The weight of it pressing down on your head is about 100 kg.

Where Rain comes from

Rain is not new water. The water which falls as rain comes from the sea, the rivers, the lakes and even from wet clothes hanging on washing lines.

These pictures show how this water becomes drops of rain or even snow flakes.

When washing dries the water does not just disappear. It becomes part of the air. Water in the air is called *water vapour*.

We say water is evaporating when it changes into water vapour. Water is evaporating from the sea, from lakes and from rivers nearly all the time.

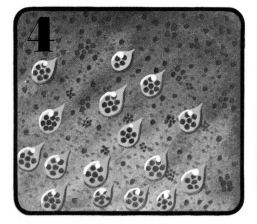

Thousands of cloud droplets join to make one rain drop. Scientists are not sure how this happens. They think perhaps the droplets collect round a speck of dust.

If it is very cold, the cloud droplets stick together and make snow flakes. Snow flakes are lots of different shapes, but each one has six sides.

Snow flakes sometimes melt and become rain before they reach the ground. Sometimes they half-melt and fall as icy rain called *sleet*.

Thunder and lightning

Thunder storm clouds are very tall, puffy and dark. Lightning is a huge spark of electricity in the clouds and thunder is the noise made by this spark.

Thunder and lightning happen at the same time. You hear the thunder after you have seen the lightning because sound travels more slowly than light.

Try counting the seconds between the lightning and the thunder. Divide this by three to work out how far away the storm is in kilometres.

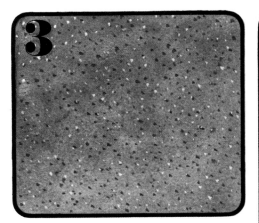

3

When the air gets colder, the vapour changes into minute droplets of water. These droplets are not heavy enough to fall as rain. They hang in the air as cloud.

Weather forecasting

This is the weather satellite, NOAA. It is a spacecraft which goes round the Earth and takes photographs of it from 1,500 km out in space. These photographs show the clouds covering the Earth. By studying them, weathermen can tell what our weather will be like.

WINGS MAKE ELECTRICITY FROM THE SUNLIGHT TO POWER THE SATELLITE

CAMERA

How to be a weather forecaster

You can get an idea of what the weather will be like by looking at the clouds.

Use this guide to help you identify the clouds in the sky. Later, note the weather they have made. You will soon know what weather to expect from different clouds.

Cirrus clouds. Very high and wispy. Warmer weather coming.

Cirrocumulus. Bands of puffy cloud across the sky. Rain coming soon.

Altocumulus. Small, puffy, white clouds high in the sky. It may rain tomorrow.

Thunder clouds. Wider at the top than the bottom. Thunder and heavy rain coming.

Tall cumulus clouds. Heavy rain very soon.

Flat cumulus clouds. Warm sunny day.

Nimbostratus. Grey cloud covering whole sky. Probably drizzle and rain soon.

Fog is cloud very near the ground.

Underground Caves

1 In some places there are huge caves and tunnels under the ground. They are usually found where the rock is *limestone*, because it is easily worn away.

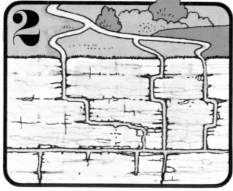

2 Limestone is a sedimentary rock, so it is made up of layers. There are cracks where the layers have broken. Water trickles down these and along between the layers.

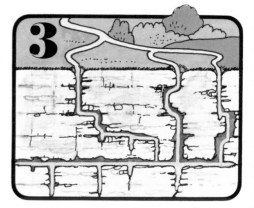

3 Limestone rock dissolves in water rather like a sugar lump does, only much more slowly. So as the water trickles through the rock it widens the cracks.

Going underground

Here are some underground caves and tunnels for you to explore.

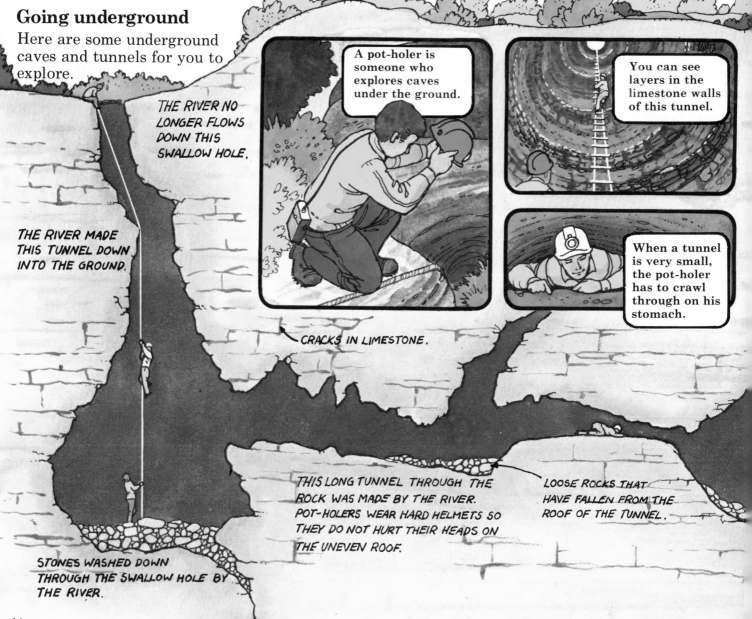

THE RIVER NO LONGER FLOWS DOWN THIS SWALLOW HOLE.

THE RIVER MADE THIS TUNNEL DOWN INTO THE GROUND.

A pot-holer is someone who explores caves under the ground.

You can see layers in the limestone walls of this tunnel.

When a tunnel is very small, the pot-holer has to crawl through on his stomach.

CRACKS IN LIMESTONE.

THIS LONG TUNNEL THROUGH THE ROCK WAS MADE BY THE RIVER. POT-HOLERS WEAR HARD HELMETS SO THEY DO NOT HURT THEIR HEADS ON THE UNEVEN ROOF.

LOOSE ROCKS THAT HAVE FALLEN FROM THE ROOF OF THE TUNNEL.

STONES WASHED DOWN THROUGH THE SWALLOW HOLE BY THE RIVER.

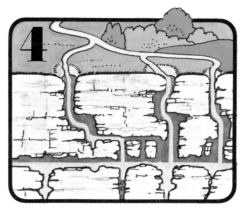

Eventually the cracks become wide tunnels and a river might flow down through them. The place where a river goes into the ground is called a *swallow hole*.

The river may flow for many kilometres under the ground. It dissolves away more of the limestone and makes the long tunnels and caves in the rock.

Discovering caves

On September 12, 1940, four boys went out hunting. They lost their dog, Robot, but they could hear him barking in a hole in the ground.

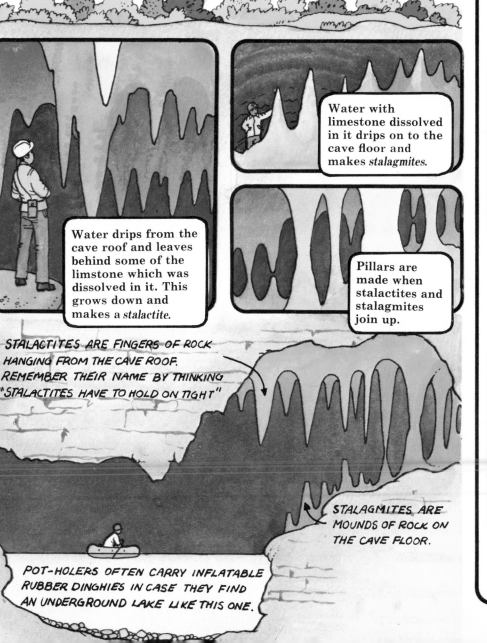

Water with limestone dissolved in it drips on to the cave floor and makes *stalagmites*.

Water drips from the cave roof and leaves behind some of the limstone which was dissolved in it. This grows down and makes a *stalactite*.

Pillars are made when stalactites and stalagmites join up.

STALACTITES ARE FINGERS OF ROCK HANGING FROM THE CAVE ROOF. REMEMBER THEIR NAME BY THINKING "STALACTITES HAVE TO HOLD ON TIGHT"

STALAGMITES ARE MOUNDS OF ROCK ON THE CAVE FLOOR.

POT-HOLERS OFTEN CARRY INFLATABLE RUBBER DINGHIES IN CASE THEY FIND AN UNDERGROUND LAKE LIKE THIS ONE.

The boys climbed down the hole to rescue Robot. They found themselves in a huge cave with paintings of animals on the walls and ceiling.

The cave the boys discovered is in Lascaux, France. The paintings were done 15,000 years ago by cavemen.

Useful Things from the Ground

The first people made tools and weapons out of stone. Later, they discovered how to get iron from rocks and make metal tools. Now people dig mines and quarries for all sorts of different rocks and metals.

Coal is a useful rock because it gives out a lot of heat when it burns. It is called a *fossil fuel* because it is made from fossilized plants. Another fossil fuel is oil, which is made from tiny sea creatures. Chemicals, candles, tar, plastics and nylon are made from oil.

Coal is made of trees which lived about 300 million years ago. The land was wet and swampy then, and covered with thick forests of trees.

The swamps were full of leaves and dead branches from the trees. The water in the swamps was very acid and this stopped the wood from rotting.

Later, the swampy land was flooded by the sea. A thick layer of sand settled at the bottom of the sea and covered the dead trees.

The dead wood was packed down very hard by the weight of the sand on top of it. Slowly it hardened to form coal.

Tunnels are dug through the ground to reach the coal, which is in layers called seams. Powerful machines cut out the coal and make tunnels in the seam.

How oil is made

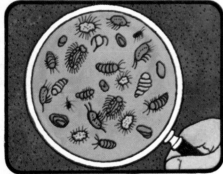

Scientists think that oil is made from tiny sea creatures like these. When these creatures die they fall to the sea floor and are buried in mud.

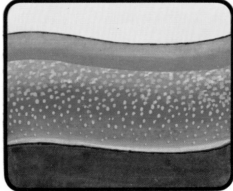

Slowly the mud hardens into rock and the creatures inside it change into little drops of oil. This takes millions of years.

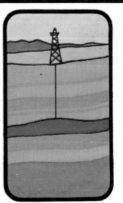

The oil which comes out of the ground is called crude oil. This is piped to refineries where it is separated into petrol and other oils.

What Happens in an Earthquake

September 1, 1923, was a hot, clear day in Tokyo, the capital city of Japan. Towards the middle of the morning people were hurrying home for lunch.

Suddenly the ground began to tremble and shake and huge cracks opened in it. People running for safety were buried as houses fell down.

Gas pipes broke and fire quickly spread through the town. Fire often causes as much damage in an earthquake as the shaking of the ground.

More than 140,000 people were killed in this earthquake. Most of them were burnt to death. Others drowned when an enormous wave flooded the ruined city.

Why earthquakes happen

Rock looks hard and brittle, but when it is under a lot of weight it will bend a bit. In parts of the Earth's crust there are strong forces slowly bending the rock.

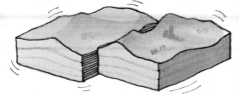

When the rock is bent too much, it suddenly snaps and the two pieces shudder and move a bit. The rocks above shake and we feel it as an *earthquake*.

Hot water from the ground

HOT ROCK

If there are hot rocks in the Earth's crust, they heat the underground water. Sometimes hot water spurts out of the ground. This is a *geyser*.

This steaming hot spring bubbles out of the ground in Iceland. Hot water is piped straight from this river to houses in the nearby town.

Volcanoes

1 On February 20, 1943, a Mexican farmer called Dionisio was ploughing his field. He heard strange rumbling noises and stopped. Then he saw smoke coming out of the ground.

2 Dionisio dropped his tools and ran. Next morning, frightened people from his village saw a smoking heap of ash in the field. It was already five times as high as a man.

3 The heap grew. By the end of the week it was 150 metres high. Hot stones, ash and steam were shooting out of the top.

A volcano cut in half

In some places the Earth's crust is thin or cracked. Here, the hot, liquid rock inside the Earth is able to force its way through the crust and form *volcanoes*.

Sometimes the hot, molten rock seeps out slowly. Sometimes there are lots of gases in the hot rock and it explodes through the crust very violently.

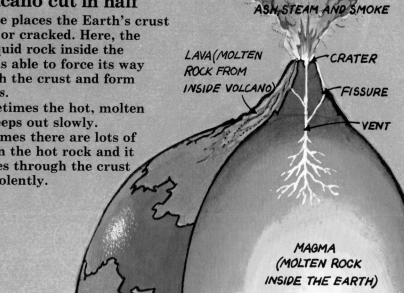

ASH, STEAM AND SMOKE

LAVA (MOLTEN ROCK FROM INSIDE VOLCANO)

CRATER

FISSURE

VENT

MAGMA (MOLTEN ROCK INSIDE THE EARTH)

Looking inside

Scientists sometimes go down inside volcanoes to find out more about them. They wear suits made of fibre-glass and aluminium to protect them from the heat.

A buried town

Mount Vesuvius in Italy had been quiet for hundreds of years. Suddenly on August 24, AD 79 it erupted violently. The nearby town of Pompeii was buried in hot lava before the people had time to get away.

Historians have dug up the remains of the town. They found body-shaped holes where the people's bodies had lain before they decayed.

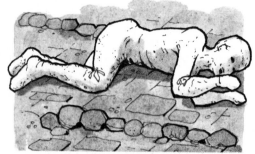

This plaster cast was made by pouring plaster into the body-shaped holes.

Bread, eggs and nuts were found in the remains of the town. They had been preserved by the lava.

4 Red-hot, liquid rock, called lava, poured out of the volcano. It buried buildings and set fire to trees. Dionisio's village was completely destroyed.

5 This volcano was named Paricutin, after Dionisio's village. A year later its lava buried a nearby town. Only the church tower was left sticking up above the lava.

How a new island was made

Volcanoes sometimes erupt in the sea. In 1963 some fishermen saw smoke rising out of the sea near Iceland. Then the top of a volcano appeared above the water. Red-hot lava poured out and it looked like a glowing fire in the sea. The volcano slowly cooled down. The new island was named Surtsey. Birds began to nest on it. Plants grew from seeds dropped by birds or washed up by the sea.

The Journey of a River

Rivers make valleys in the hills and help shape the countryside. Their water comes from rain and melted snow. If there is not much rain, the rivers dry up.

Follow this river on its journey from the hills to the sea and find out what happens to it on the way.

A river does not flow straight. It swings from side to side and cuts a winding valley. The pieces of hill sticking out across the valley are called *spurs*.

Rain water drains into streams.

Lots of streams join to make a river.

This is a spur. Look at picture ① on the left to find out more about it.

The place where a river begins is called its source.

Some rain water soaks through the ground and bubbles out as a spring many kilometres away.

A river which flows into another river is called a tributary.

Some waterfalls are made when a river flows over a hard rock onto a softer one. The softer rock wears away and makes a step. The water then tumbles over the step.

Loops in the river are called *meanders*. After a while, the river may break its banks and flow straight on. The loop it leaves behind is called an *ox-bow lake*.

Water in the ground

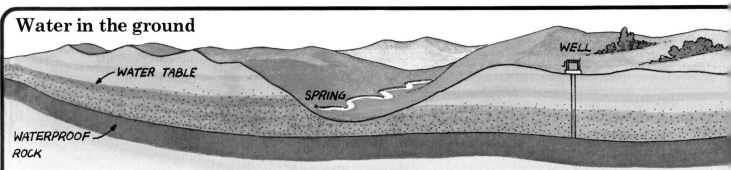

Rain water soaks through the ground until it reaches a waterproof rock. This sort of rock is too solid for water to trickle through.

The rocks above the waterproof rock hold water rather like a sponge does. The top of the water in them is called the *water table*.

A hole dug down through the water table soon fills with water. This is how a well is made.

The place where a river flows into the sea is called its mouth.

The river drops all of its load of sand and mud when it flows into the sea. If the sea does not wash it away it builds up to make a *delta* like this.

This is a meander. Find out more about it from picture ③ on the left.

When the river floods, it spreads mud over the land. This makes good soil for plants to grow in.

Look at picture ② to find out how a waterfall is made.

The river flows more slowly on flatter land and drops some of the stones it is carrying.

A river carries lots of stones, sand and mud in its water. This is called its load.

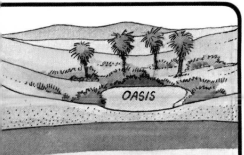

OASIS

There is water under the ground even in the desert. If there is a dip in the ground and the water table is near the surface, it makes an *oasis*.

Power from rivers

Flowing water is very powerful. People used to build mills by rivers and use the water to turn a mill wheel. This drove the machinery for grinding corn.

Water can be used to drive the machines which make electricity. A river is dammed and the water is piped to the power station.

Going up a Mountain

As you climb higher up a mountain you feel colder and colder. Even in very hot places, you will find snow on the mountains if you climb high enough.

Winter high in the mountains is bitterly cold. The ground is covered with snow for most of the year. Only special mountain plants that can stand the cold are able to grow there.

Follow the climber in these pictures and see how the mountainside changes as you climb higher.

The kind of trees that grow furthest up a mountain are *conifers*. They have stiff, needle-shaped leaves which help the trees survive the cold weather.

Suddenly, the trees end. They do not grow further up the mountain because it is too cold. This height is called the *tree line*. Above it, there is only grass.

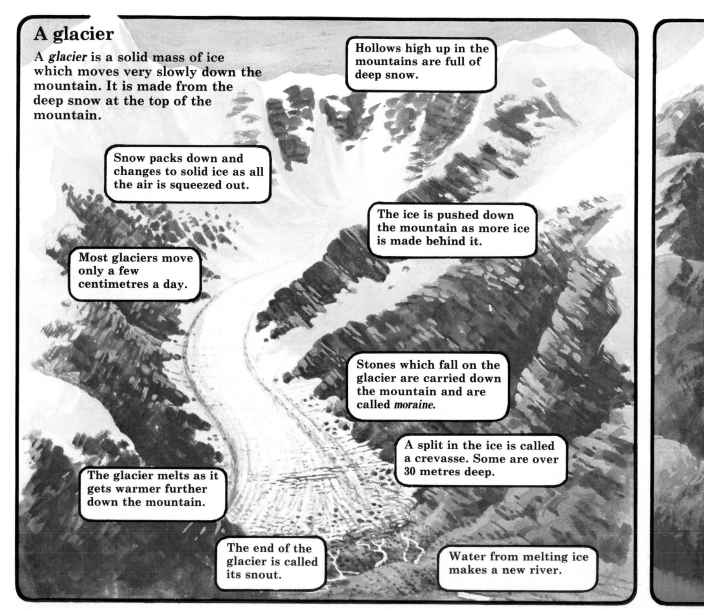

A glacier

A *glacier* is a solid mass of ice which moves very slowly down the mountain. It is made from the deep snow at the top of the mountain.

Hollows high up in the mountains are full of deep snow.

Snow packs down and changes to solid ice as all the air is squeezed out.

The ice is pushed down the mountain as more ice is made behind it.

Most glaciers move only a few centimetres a day.

Stones which fall on the glacier are carried down the mountain and are called *moraine*.

A split in the ice is called a crevasse. Some are over 30 metres deep.

The glacier melts as it gets warmer further down the mountain.

The end of the glacier is called its snout.

Water from melting ice makes a new river.

3 Higher up still, the mountain is rocky and bare. The air feels cold and there are patches of snow even in summer. Tiny flowers grow during the warmer months.

4 Now you have reached the *snow line*. Above here the mountain is always covered with snow. The snow is very deep and nothing can grow here.

Snow slides

People who live in high mountains know that the snow may suddenly slip off the steep mountain slope. When this happens, it is called an *avalanche*.

2 A sudden noise or movement—somebody shouting perhaps—can start the snow slipping. Masses of snow slide down the mountain and bury everything on the way.

3 Special dogs are trained to find people buried in an avalanche. The dogs sniff the snow till they find someone. Then they dig them out with their paws.

After a glacier has melted

Thousands of years ago the weather was very cold. There were more glaciers than there are now. When the ice melted, the glaciers left valleys which looked like this.

The hollow where the glacier started is called a cirque.

The glacier carved this deep, steep-sided valley.

This valley was dug by a smaller glacier. It is not as deep as the main valley.

The river cascades over a waterfall to the main valley.

This hill is made of stones dropped by the glacier. It is called a moraine.

The moraine dammed the river so the river flooded the valley and made this lake.

Eventually the river will wear a channel through the moraine. Then the lake will drain away.

Hot and Cold Places

These pictures take you on a trip from the North Pole to the equator.

The Poles are the coldest places on Earth. As you travel down from the North Pole, each place you visit is warmer than the last. The landscape changes with the weather.

Places on the equator are always hot. After you have passed the equator, the weather begins to get cooler again. It gets colder and colder then until you reach the South Pole.

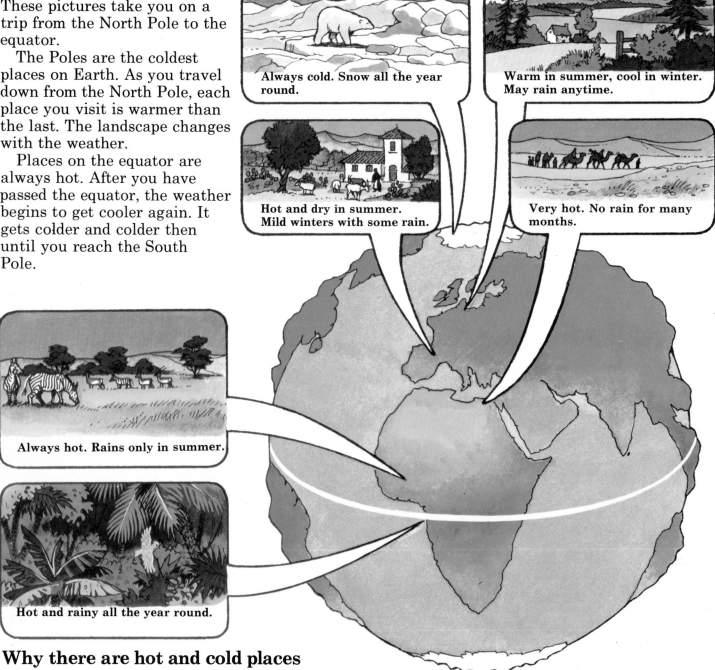

Always cold. Snow all the year round.

Warm in summer, cool in winter. May rain anytime.

Hot and dry in summer. Mild winters with some rain.

Very hot. No rain for many months.

Always hot. Rains only in summer.

Hot and rainy all the year round.

Why there are hot and cold places

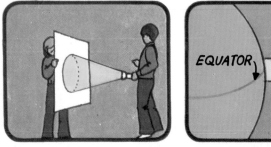

SUN'S RAYS

EQUATOR

NORTH POLE

SUN'S RAYS

A torch shining straight at a piece of card makes a small, but very bright, patch of light. The Sun's rays are like this at the equator and make it very hot there.

When the card is tilted, the patch of light is much bigger but paler. The Sun's rays are like this at the Poles. Each ray spreads out very thinly and so does not heat the land much.

Hot Dry Places

Deserts are the driest places in the world. They sometimes have no rain for several years. Cactus plants can live there because they store water in their stalks.

Not all deserts are sandy. In some, the ground is rocky with very little soil. Wind and sudden rain storms wear the rock into these strange shapes.

In a sandy desert, the wind heaps sand into little hills called *dunes*. The dunes move forward as sand is blown up the gentle slope and slips over the steep side.

There is water in the ground even though it hardly ever rains. If this water reaches the surface, it makes an oasis. Date trees and other plants grow round the pool.

After a sudden rain storm, the desert is covered with flowers. Their seeds lie in the sand until there is enough water for them to grow.

Camels can live for several days without any water. They get very thin and then drink as much as 20 buckets of water at a time.

Hot Wet Places

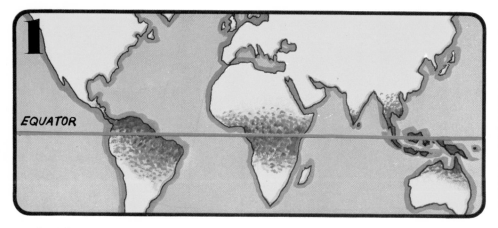

1

Most of the land round the equator is covered with thick, very green forest, called *rain forest*. It rains heavily nearly every day and there are often thunder storms.

The air is hot and steamy. The plants there like the heat and wetness, and grow very large, with lots of fruit and flowers.

2

Places near the equator do not have summer and winter. They stay in the Sun's hottest rays all year round, so the weather never gets cold.

3

Inside the rain forest it is dark and shady. Some of the trees are higher than a ten-storey office block. They have thick trunks with huge roots to support them.

4

The trees are like big umbrellas, keeping most of the sunlight out of the forest. A thick tangle of plants fights for any light that seeps through to the forest floor.

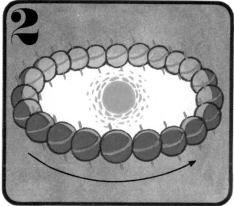

5

Plants with long, rope-like stems hang from the trees. They are called lianas. The stems are strong and are sometimes used for making rope bridges.

6

The easiest way to travel through rain forest is to follow a river. The trees and lianas grow so thickly along the river banks that you cannot see into the forest.

7

Rain forest is always green and there are brightly coloured fruits and flowers all year round. The trees do not all lose their leaves at the same time because there is no cold season.

Most of the animals that live in the forest can climb or fly. They need to be able to reach food that grows very high up.

Icy Places

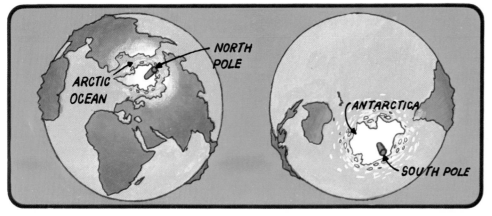

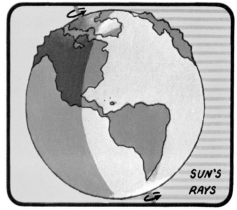

Thick ice covers the North and South Poles all the year. There is no land at the North Pole. An enormous slab of ice floats on the Arctic Ocean.

At the South Pole, the ice covers a big piece of land called Antarctica. Daylight at the Poles lasts for six months at a time. It is dark for the rest of the year.

The Poles do not move in and out of the sunlight when the Earth spins round. This is because the Earth is tilted. One Pole is in daylight, while the other is dark.

At the South Pole

The land at the South Pole was discovered only 150 years ago.

In winter, the sea round Antarctica is frozen. Some of the ice melts in summer. Then, strongly built ships called icebreakers can push their way through to the land.

The only people who live in Antarctica are scientists. They study the rocks and the ice there. The ice is so deep that only the tops of high mountains stick up above it.

Scientists have found coal in the rocks under the snow. Coal is made from trees, so Antarctica must once have been warm enough for trees to grow.

Penguins and other birds live by the sea and catch fish. Further inland, the largest animal is a fly. There are no other animals because there is nothing for them to eat.

Seals and whales live in the sea round Antarctica. They move north when the sea freezes. These animals have a thick layer of fat under their skin which helps to keep them warm.

Antarctica is sometimes called a cold desert because it is so bare and lifeless. A few tiny plants such as mosses grow where there is no ice.

How a Town Grows

Hundreds of years ago most of our towns were small villages. The remains of the villages were buried as new houses and roads were built. Sometimes, people dig up clues which help us to piece together the history of a town.

The first villages were built where people could grow their food. They needed good soil and a spring for water. They looked for a place they could defend from their enemies.

This is the story of how villages grow into towns.

Looking at towns

This is a town we have made up. In many ways it is probably like towns you know. Most towns have houses, shops and offices, factories, roads and bridges. The houses and streets may look different, but can you see how this town is like towns you know?

Food grown to feed people working in town.

By-pass road round town keeps traffic out of town centre.

Playing fields on flat land near town.

Market place in old town.

These walls were built to protect the old town from enemies.

Sports stadium in new part of town.

Old bridge.

Modern town has spread to this side of river.

Power station makes electricity for town.

The first people on Earth probably did not build houses. They wandered over the countryside, hunting animals and picking berries to eat, and slept in caves.

Later, people learnt how to plant seeds and grow food. They tamed wild animals so they did not need to hunt. They settled in one place, built houses and tended the farms.

At first people only grew food for themselves. Later, they grew fruit and vegetables to sell. Some villages became market towns where people did their shopping.

About 200 years ago, lots of factories were built near iron and coal mines. Large towns grew up as people moved to work in the new factories.

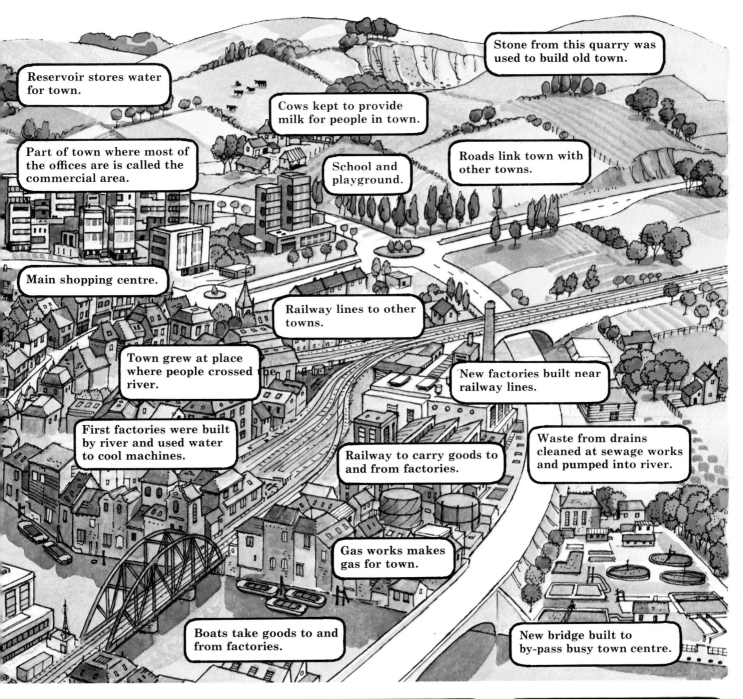

Reservoir stores water for town.

Stone from this quarry was used to build old town.

Cows kept to provide milk for people in town.

Part of town where most of the offices are is called the commercial area.

School and playground.

Roads link town with other towns.

Main shopping centre.

Railway lines to other towns.

Town grew at place where people crossed the river.

New factories built near railway lines.

First factories were built by river and used water to cool machines.

Railway to carry goods to and from factories.

Waste from drains cleaned at sewage works and pumped into river.

Gas works makes gas for town.

Boats take goods to and from factories.

New bridge built to by-pass busy town centre.

5 The first settlements by the sea were fishing villages. When people began to travel and sell goods to other countries, some villages grew into huge seaports.

6 Some towns in the mountains or by the sea have become holiday resorts. These towns have lots of hotels, restaurants and shops to serve the holidaymakers.

7 This is a ghost town. The people left because there was no work for them. This happened to many gold-mining towns when all the gold had gone.

Rock Spotter's Guide

There are hundreds of different kinds of rocks, but every rock is either sedimentary, igneous or metamorphic.

You might like to try and identify a piece of rock. These are some of the things to look for in it.

1. Can you see layers?
2. Are there any fossils?
3. Does it feel rough or glassy?
4. Is it made up of tiny grains?
5. Is it a very hard rock?

Here are some of the more common rocks you might find.

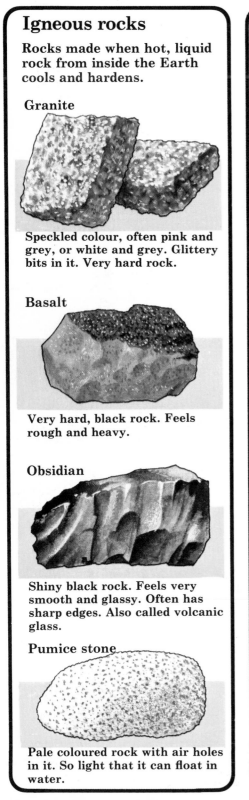

Igneous rocks

Rocks made when hot, liquid rock from inside the Earth cools and hardens.

Granite

Speckled colour, often pink and grey, or white and grey. Glittery bits in it. Very hard rock.

Basalt

Very hard, black rock. Feels rough and heavy.

Obsidian

Shiny black rock. Feels very smooth and glassy. Often has sharp edges. Also called volcanic glass.

Pumice stone

Pale coloured rock with air holes in it. So light that it can float in water.

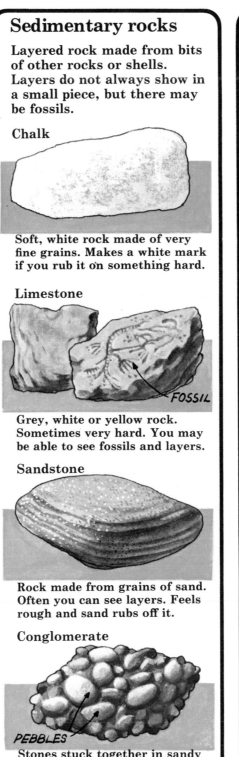

Sedimentary rocks

Layered rock made from bits of other rocks or shells. Layers do not always show in a small piece, but there may be fossils.

Chalk

Soft, white rock made of very fine grains. Makes a white mark if you rub it on something hard.

Limestone

FOSSIL

Grey, white or yellow rock. Sometimes very hard. You may be able to see fossils and layers.

Sandstone

Rock made from grains of sand. Often you can see layers. Feels rough and sand rubs off it.

Conglomerate

PEBBLES

Stones stuck together in sandy rock. The stones are often smooth, rounded pebbles.

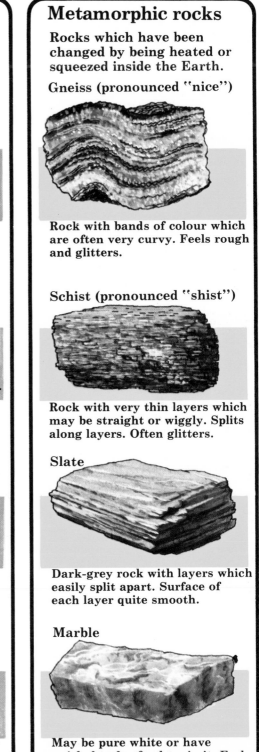

Metamorphic rocks

Rocks which have been changed by being heated or squeezed inside the Earth.

Gneiss (pronounced "nice")

Rock with bands of colour which are often very curvy. Feels rough and glitters.

Schist (pronounced "shist")

Rock with very thin layers which may be straight or wiggly. Splits along layers. Often glitters.

Slate

Dark-grey rock with layers which easily split apart. Surface of each layer quite smooth.

Marble

May be pure white or have swirly bands of colour in it. Feels rough and grainy.

Earth Words

Atmosphere
Blanket of air 550 km thick round the Earth.

Axis
Line through the middle of the Earth from north to south.

Core
Centre of the Earth. Probably made of very hot, liquid metal.

Crater (Moon)
Hollows on the Moon's surface.

Crater (Volcano)
Hollow in a volcano where the molten rock comes out.

Crust
Earth's shell of solid rock up to 64 km thick.

Delta
Land made from sand, mud and stones dropped by a river when it flows into the sea.

Desert
Land which is so dry that very few plants can grow.

Earthquake
The shuddering and cracking of the Earth caused by rocks moving deep in the Earth.

Equator
Line round the widest part of the Earth.

Fossil
Shape preserved in rock, of an animal or plant which lived long ago.

Galaxy
A group of hundreds of millions of stars.

Geyser
A fountain of hot water which spurts up from under the ground.

Glacier
A mass of ice moving slowly down a mountain.

Hemisphere
Half a sphere. The two halves of the Earth are called the northern hemisphere and the southern hemisphere.

Igneous rock
Rock made when hot, liquid rock from inside the Earth cools and hardens.

Magma
The hot, liquid rock inside the Earth.

Mantle
The part of the Earth which is made of hot, liquid rock.

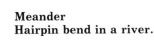
Meander
Hairpin bend in a river.

Metamorphic rock
Rock which has been changed by being heated or squeezed inside the Earth.

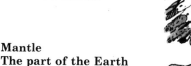
Moon
A ball of rock in space which goes round a planet.

Oasis
Place in a desert where the water in the ground reaches the surface and plants can grow.

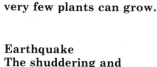
Ox-bow lake
Lake made from the bit of a river left when a river breaks its banks and stops flowing round a bend.

Planet
A ball of rock or gas which goes round a star and does not give out light.

Plate
One piece of the Earth's crust.

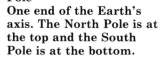
Pole
One end of the Earth's axis. The North Pole is at the top and the South Pole is at the bottom.

Satellite
A moon or other object in space which goes round a planet or star.

Sedimentary rock
Rock made from pieces of other rocks or shells.

Snow line
Height above which there is snow all the year on a mountain.

Spur
The part of a hill which sticks across a valley at a bend in a river.

Stalactite
Fingers of rock on the roof of a limestone cave.

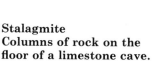
Stalagmite
Columns of rock on the floor of a limestone cave.

Star
A ball of gases in space which gives out heat and light.

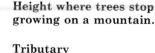
Tree line
Height where trees stop growing on a mountain.

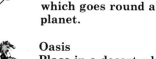
Tributary
A river which flows into another river.

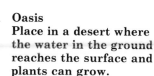
Volcano
Place where hot, liquid rock breaks through the Earth's crust.

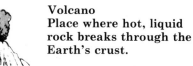

Earth Facts

Earth measurements

12,713 km

12,756 km

EQUATOR

The Earth is not a completely round ball. It is slightly flattened at the Poles. So the line through the Earth from Pole to Pole is not as long as a line through the Earth at the equator.

The distance all the way round the equator is 40,075 km.

The Earth is going round the Sun. It is travelling at a speed of 107,200 k.p.h. It takes $365\frac{1}{4}$ days to complete one trip round the Sun.

The Earth is spinning round its axis. It takes 23 hours, 56 minutes and 4 seconds to spin round once. A place on the equator is moving at a speed of about 1,600 k.p.h.

The highest on Earth

The highest mountain is Mount Everest, on the border of Tibet and Nepal. Its summit is 8848 m above sea level.

The highest waterfall is the Angel Falls in Venezuela, South America. The water cascades down 979 m.

The tallest stalagmite is 29 m high. It is in Lozère, France and is called *La Grande Stalagmite*.

The longest stalactite hangs 59 m down from the roof of a cave near Malaga, Spain.

The highest active volcano is 6,100 m high. It is the Volcan Antofalla in Argentina.

The highest a geyser has ever spurted is 457 m. This was the Waimangu geyser in New Zealand in 1904.

The longest on Earth

The longest rivers are the Nile in Africa and the Amazon in South America. The Nile is 6,670 km long and the Amazon is 6,448 km long.

The longest lightning ever measured was 32 km.

The longest flows of lava are in Iceland. The lava has flowed 96 km from the crater of the volcano.

The longest glacier is the Lambert Glacier in Antarctica. It is 402 km long and 64 km wide.

Hottest and wettest

The highest temperature ever recorded is 59.4°c. It was in Algeria in 1973.

The lowest temperature ever recorded is −88.3°c. It was in Vostok, Antarctica, in 1960.

The wettest place in the world is Mount Wai-'ale'ale on Hawaii. An average of 11.45 m of rain falls every year.

The most rain to fall in one day is 1.87 m on the island of La Reunion in the Indian Ocean.

The driest place in the world is in the Atacama desert in Chile. It rained in 1971 for the first time in about 400 years.

The deepest on Earth

The deepest ocean is the Pacific and the deepest part of the ocean ever measured is more than 11 km deep.

The deepest hole drilled into the Earth's crust is 9.58 km deep. It is a natural gas well in Oklahoma, U.S.A.

The deepest lake is Lake Baykal in the U.S.S.R. It is 1,940 m deep.

The lowest land in the world is round the Dead Sea. It is 393 m below sea level.

Volcanoes and earthquakes

There are 535 active volcanoes in the world and about 80 of them are under the sea.
The greatest number of active volcanoes is in Indonesia.
There is even an active volcano in Antarctica. It is called Mount Erebus.

Every year there are about 500,000 earthquakes. Of these, 100,000 are strong enough to be felt and 1,000 cause damage.

Part Two
The Seas Around Us

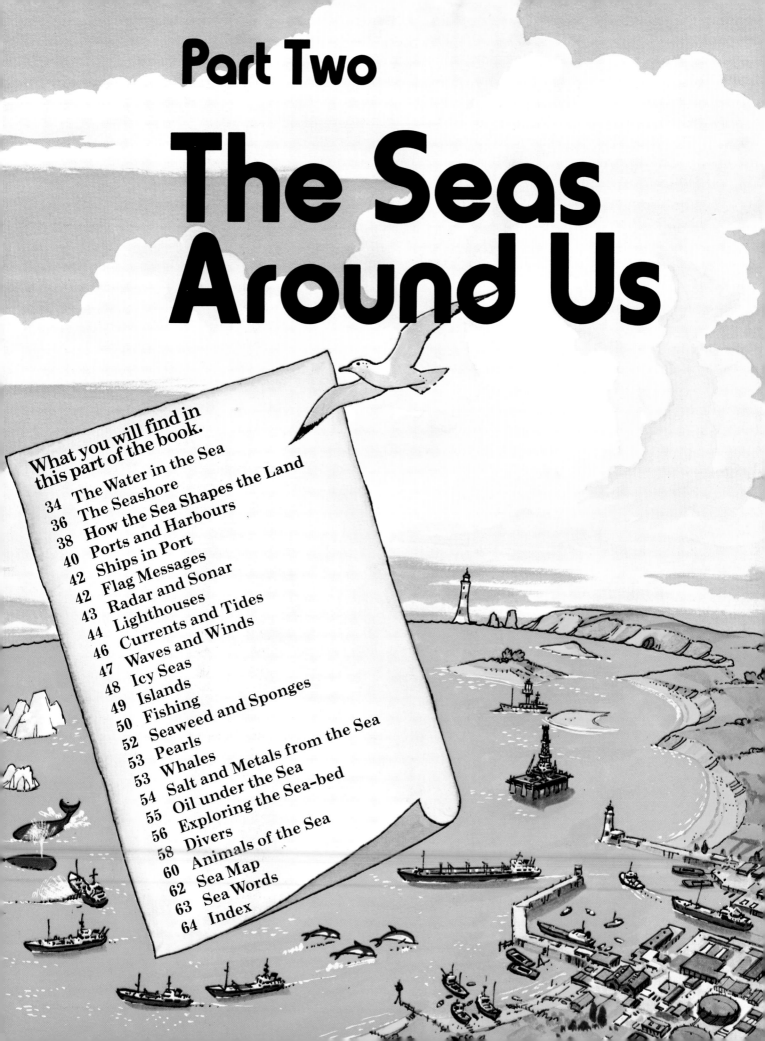

What you will find in this part of the book.

The Water in the Sea

About seven-tenths of the Earth's surface is covered by sea, yet once there were no seas at all. Scientists think that about 3,500 million years ago the Earth was very hot and surrounded by clouds of steam.

As the Earth cooled, so did the steam around it. You may have noticed how steam on a cold window changes into trickles of water. This is what happened to the steam around the Earth. The water from it made seas in the hollows in the Earth's surface.

1 The sea and the land

If all the water in the seas could be drained away, the surface of the Earth would look something like this. Some of the mountains would be twice as high as Everest.

Imagine all the water being poured back again. It fills the landscape almost to the top. The bits left sticking up out of the water are what we call land.

A water trail

The world's water is always on the move from one place to another. Follow the water trail round this picture to find out how it moves.

3 The air gets colder higher up. The water vapour up here changes into tiny water droplets which hang together as cloud.

1 START HERE. Tiny specks of water, too small to see, are leaving the sea all the time. They become part of the air and are called *water vapour.*

2 When water changes into water vapour, we say it is *evaporating.* Evaporation happens more quickly when the Sun shines strongly.

Why the seas are salty

Rivers dissolve lots of chemicals out of the rocks and wash them into the sea. One of these chemicals is the salt we eat with our food. When the sea water evaporates, the salt is left behind in the sea. This is why the sea tastes salty.

9 Rivers flow downhill until they reach the sea. Mud, sand and stones that they have carried with them, are dumped on the sea-bed and can sometimes be seen as sandbanks. GO BACK TO START.

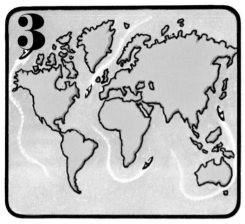

3

This map shows the world's great oceans. The seas and oceans are all joined up and you can travel from one to the other without crossing any land.

4

1,000 METRES ABOVE SEA LEVEL

SEA LEVEL.

Because all the seas are joined the water reaches about the same height up the land all the way round the world. This height is called sea level.

5

1 2 3 4 5 6 7 8 9

Imagine we could rearrange a world map and put all the land together at one end and all the seas at the other. It would look something like this. It shows you how much of the Earth is covered by sea.

4 The wind blows the clouds across the sky.

6 If it is very cold, the cloud droplets freeze and fall as snowflakes.

5 The tiny cloud-water droplets join together—scientists are not sure how—and fall as raindrops.

7 On high mountains, there is snow all year round. Little streams of melted snow run down the mountainside.

8 Other streams are fed by rain water. The streams and small rivers flow into big rivers.

The Seashore

The place where the sea washes the land is called the *shore*. Sometimes the shore is rocky, or it may be a beach made of sand or pebbles.

Near the land the waves in the sea grow taller and then break on the shore in a mass of white foam. The pounding of the waves wears away the rocks and shapes the shoreline.

On most shores there is a *tide*. This is the movement of the sea in and out over the land. At low tide the beach is left bare.

1 How waves break

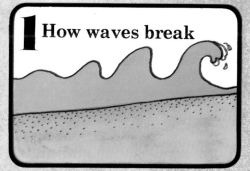

In shallow water the bottom of the wave drags along the ground. The top of the wave moves faster, curls over and breaks off from the bottom of the wave.

2 PLUNGING BREAKER

When the beach is very steep the waves curl right over at the top and then crash down with a lot of noise and spray. These are called plunging breakers.

3 SPILLING BREAKER   GOOD WAVES FOR SURFING.

On flat beaches the waves break more gently. Foam spills down the front of the wave from a little curl at the top.

At the seaside

These pictures show some of the things you might see on the seashore.

1 Boulders

The waves beat against the cliffs and slowly wear away the rocks. At the foot of the cliffs there are big rocks which have broken off the cliffs.

2 Small pebbles

Small stones are carried in the waves. They bang and grind against each other and slowly they become smooth and rounded. Then they are called pebbles.

3 Sand

Sand is lots of tiny bits of very hard rock. Softer rock wears away to become fine mud. Often there are little chips of sea-shell in the sand too.

ROCK POOLS ARE TRAPPED HERE WHEN THE TIDE GOES OUT.

1

BOULDERS

BREAKING WAVES

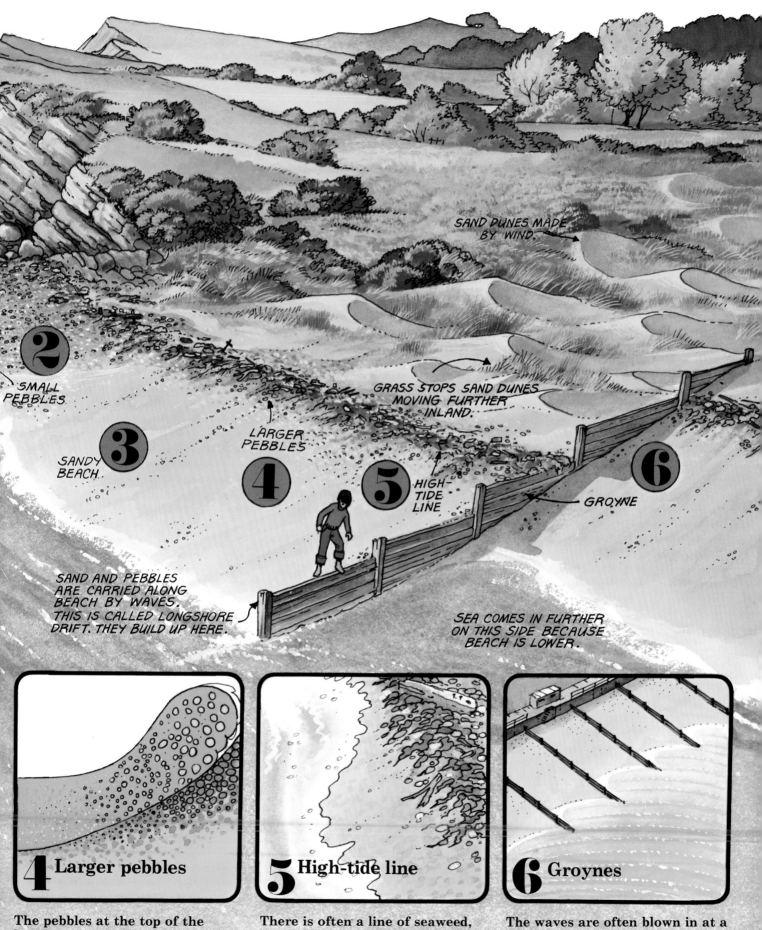

2 SMALL PEBBLES.

3 SANDY BEACH.

4 LARGER PEBBLES

5 HIGH-TIDE LINE

6 GROYNE

SAND DUNES MADE BY WIND.

GRASS STOPS SAND DUNES MOVING FURTHER INLAND.

SAND AND PEBBLES ARE CARRIED ALONG BEACH BY WAVES. THIS IS CALLED LONGSHORE DRIFT. THEY BUILD UP HERE.

SEA COMES IN FURTHER ON THIS SIDE BECAUSE BEACH IS LOWER.

4 Larger pebbles

The pebbles at the top of the beach are larger than those further down. The waves sweep them up there but cannot carry them back again.

5 High-tide line

There is often a line of seaweed, shells and litter along the beach. This has been left stranded by the waves when the tide went out. It is called the high tide line.

6 Groynes

The waves are often blown in at a slant to the shore. Walls, called groynes, are built to stop the sand and pebbles being carried along the shore by these waves.

How the Sea Shapes the Land

Waves are pounding the seashore all the time. They hammer against the cliffs and slowly wear them away. Bits of rock are broken off and then picked up by the next wave and hurled back against the cliff-face.

As the waves crash down on the rocks, air is trapped underneath them. This air is forced into cracks in the rock, splitting them open even more.

In some places the land is being worn away so quickly that walls have to be built to protect it.

1 How land is eaten away

Sometimes the waves wear away the bottom of cliffs and the top is left hanging. It is never safe to go near the edge of cliffs because the land might crumble away.

2 **3**

As cliffs are worn back, roads and even towns may fall into the sea. About 600 years ago there was a busy town called Dunwich, on the east coast of England.

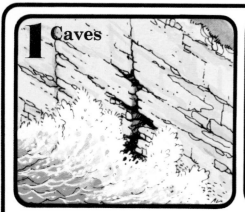

1 Caves

Cracks in the rock are worn away more quickly than the rest of the cliff. The waves slam into the cracks and slowly widen them and make them into caves.

2

The waves thunder into the cave and break against the cave walls. Water dashes against the cave roof and sometimes wears a hole right through it.

3

The hole in the roof of a cave is called a blowhole. As the waves break in the cave below, spray spurts up out of the blowhole.

4

Later, the pounding of the waves inside the cave might make the whole roof fall in. Then the cave becomes a narrow inlet in the cliffs.

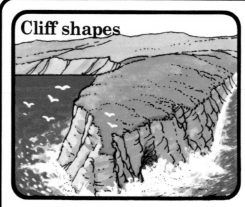

Cliff shapes

Rocky headlands are attacked on all sides by the waves. Cracks in the rock are widened as the waves break against the headland. Some of the cracks become caves.

Caves can form on both sides of the headland, back-to-back. The waves break down the back of the caves and make an arch through the headland.

The cliffs slowly crumbled away and whole buildings fell into the sea. Now only the graveyard remains and, with each storm, more graves fall into the sea.

Bays and coves

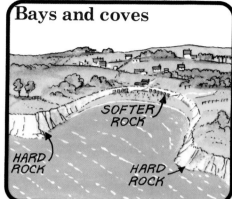

Hard rocks stand up to the waves better than softer rocks. The softer rocks are worn back to make bays while the harder rocks stick out as headlands.

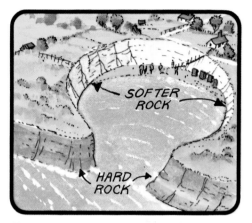

This is a cove. The sea has broken through a ridge of hard rock and is eating away the softer rock behind it. Inside the cove, the sea is calm because it is sheltered.

Land made by the sea

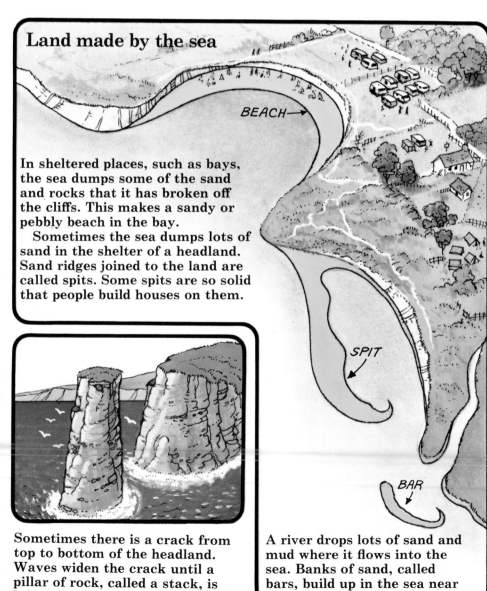

In sheltered places, such as bays, the sea dumps some of the sand and rocks that it has broken off the cliffs. This makes a sandy or pebbly beach in the bay.

Sometimes the sea dumps lots of sand in the shelter of a headland. Sand ridges joined to the land are called spits. Some spits are so solid that people build houses on them.

Sometimes there is a crack from top to bottom of the headland. Waves widen the crack until a pillar of rock, called a stack, is left standing alone in the sea.

A river drops lots of sand and mud where it flows into the sea. Banks of sand, called bars, build up in the sea near the mouth of the river.

Rock shapes made by the sea

Hard rocks wear down evenly on all sides. They become very rounded pebbles. You might find pebbles that are almost as round as marbles.

Flat pebbles come from rocks which are made up of layers. You can sometimes see the layers as bands of different colour in the pebbles.

Ports and Harbours

People need places to keep their ships and boats when they are not at sea. These places must be sheltered from wind and rough seas so that the ships are not damaged and can be loaded and unloaded easily.

Such places are called *harbours*. Some parts of the coast make good natural harbours. Other harbours have to be specially built. Warehouses and factories are built round the harbour and the whole area is called a *port*.

Dredgers

Harbours are sheltered places with calm water, so sand and mud settle on the bottom. To keep the harbour deep, the sand has to be dug up by dredgers.

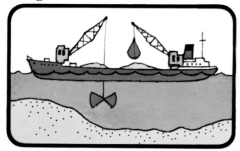

This is a grab dredger. It digs up sand from the harbour bottom and dumps it in a barge. In some harbours, extra-deep channels are made for really big ships.

A bucket dredger has lots of buckets on a belt which goes round and round. Each bucket scoops up sand, and then tips it down a chute into a barge.

1 Why harbours are where they are

A good place for a harbour is in the mouth of a river. Here the water is sheltered by the land. Sometimes the river has to be made deeper for big ships.

2

Another sheltered place is a bay protected by high cliffs. A concrete pier is sometimes built across the entrance to the bay to keep out rough waves.

Look round a harbour

Here are some of the things you might see in a large harbour.

Dock for passenger ships.

Concrete platform, called a *quay*, where ships are tied up.

Quay cranes for loading and unloading the ships.

Tugs help big ships into position alongside the quay.

Dock

Dry dock. Water is pumped out so ships can be mended or painted.

Posts, called bollards, for ships to tie up to.

Lock gates to keep water in dock at the same level all the time.

River. Water level goes up and down here with the tides.

How a lock works

In a small fishing harbour the boats are often left high and dry when the tide goes out. They can leave the harbour only when the tide comes in again.

Big harbours have lock gates to keep the water in when the tide goes out. Without the gates the water would go up and down and make ship-loading difficult.

A *lock* has two sets of gates with a short channel of water between. To enter the harbour the ship goes into the channel and the gates are closed behind it.

Now the level of the water in the lock has to be made the same as in the harbour. Water is let in to the lock through small gates called sluices.

Special cranes for unloading container ships.

Railway for carrying goods to and from the docks.

Swing-bridge moved out of the way so a ship can go through.

Barges

Lorries carry goods to and from docks.

Oil storage tanks

Rails for cranes to move along quay.

Oil tanker

Warehouses for storing cargo.

Ship being guided along deep water channel.

As the water level in the lock rises, the ship floats up with it. When it is the same height as the harbour water, the gates are opened and the ship moves out.

Ships in Port

Here you can see how different types of ships are dealt with when they come into port.

This is a general cargo ship which carries goods of all shapes and sizes. Quayside cranes fitted with hooks or slings are used to load and unload it.

Container ships only carry goods that have been packed into big boxes called containers. Special cranes like this one are used to lift the containers on and off.

When oil tankers dock, they are joined on to pipelines. The oil is then pumped through these pipes to storage tanks on land. The tankers are also filled in this way.

Wheat and sugar are sometimes carried loose in big, bulk-carrier ships. They are poured down chutes into the ship and sucked out again by pipes.

Some ships are built so that vehicles can drive on and off them. They are used for ferrying lorries, trains and cars, and are called roll on/roll off ships, or RO/RO's.

Ships with cranes on deck can unload into barges. These can take the cargo to towns further up river, without unloading it in the harbour first.

Flag Messages

Ships usually have flags flying from their masts. These are not to make the ship look pretty, they are used for sending messages.

Sailors have a code with one flag for each letter. Strings of flags are flown to spell out messages. Most ships have country and company flags too.

Here are some of the flags in the code. One or two flags, flying by themselves, have special meanings.

Letter "A".
Can mean "Be careful, I have a diver down".

Letter "B".
Or, "I am carrying explosives".

Letter "G".
Or, "I need a pilot to help me into harbour".

Letter "P".
Or, "Ship about to sail, everyone must come aboard". This flag is called Blue Peter.

Letter "W".
Or, "I need medical help".

FLAG OF COMPANY WHICH OWNS SHIP.

FLAG OF COUNTRY WHOSE PORT THE SHIP IS IN.

MESSAGE: "I NEED HELP".

MESSAGE: "I AM NOT MOVING".

FLAG OF SHIP'S OWN COUNTRY

Radar and Sonar

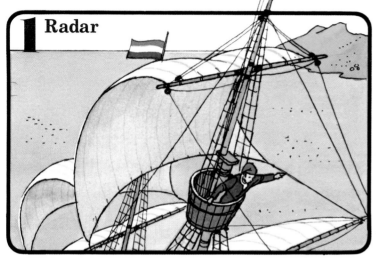

1 Radar

Ships used to have look-outs at the top of the mast to warn the captain of approaching ships or land. This worked well if it was a clear day.

2

RADAR SCANNER SPINNING ROUND.

When it was dark or foggy, look-outs were not much use. Modern ships have *radar* instead. They send out a kind of radio wave in all directions.

3

If the radar waves hit another ship, they bounce back like an echo. We have shown the waves in white so you can see them, but really they are invisible.

4

The radar scanner collects the echo and makes a dot on a special television screen on the ship's bridge.

The ship's navigator works out where the other ship is from the position of the dot on the screen. Then, if necessary, he changes his course to make sure he does not hit it.

5

Radar waves also bounce back from the land and from aeroplanes. Aeroplanes often have radar of their own too.

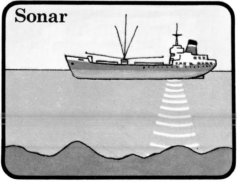

Sonar

Some ships have equipment called *sonar* which sends out sound waves. These are echoed back by the sea-bed, submarines or even by shoals of fish.

A ship's lights show which way it is pointing at night. It has a green light on its right (*starboard*) side and a red light on its left (*port*) side.

43

Lighthouses

1. Lighthouses through history

People have used lights to warn ships of dangerous coastlines for centuries. At first, the lights were just bonfires lit on the tops of hills.

2.

Towers were built so that the light from the fire could be seen from further away. Some early lighthouses were built of wood, but these often burnt down.

3.

Later lighthouses used candles, coal fires and oil lamps for their light. Now most have electric lights and their towers are made of stone or metal.

4.

When there is no solid rock to build a lighthouse on, lightships are used. They mark sandbanks and reefs and must be securely anchored to withstand rough seas.

5.

Some lightships have been replaced by light towers. The long pole is joined to a platform which stands on the sea-bed. These are safer than lightships.

6.

This is a new kind of warning light called a LANBY. Its light and foghorn work automatically, so no-one has to live on it. It is towed into position by tugs.

Buoys

Buoys are coloured metal floats which are anchored to the sea-bed. They warn ships of dangerous rocks, sandbanks or wrecks and mark the safe channels.

Some buoys have rings on top. These are for ships to tie up to, perhaps while waiting to go into harbour. Big mooring buoys are steady enough to stand on.

Inside a lighthouse

Here is a lighthouse built on a rock a little way out to sea. We have taken away part of the wall so that you can see inside. The light warns ships of the dangerous rocks around it. Three lighthouse keepers live here for a month at a time.

Life on a lighthouse

Labels on the lighthouse diagram:

LIGHT

SERVICE ROOM WITH LIGHT AND FOGHORN CONTROLS.

STAIRS

BEDROOM. BUNKS ARE CURVED TO FIT ROUND WALLS.

LIVING-ROOM AND KITCHEN.

BATTERIES TO POWER LIGHT IN EMERGENCIES.

OIL FOR POWERING MACHINERY AND COOKER.

2½ METRE THICK WALLS.

GENERATOR WHICH MAKES ELECTRICITY FOR THE LIGHT.

STRIPES MAKE LIGHTHOUSE SHOW UP DURING THE DAY.

FRESH WATER TANKS

1 Life on a lighthouse

2

Every morning, two keepers clean the windows, lenses and light and check all the machinery to make sure it is working properly. The third keeper cooks lunch.

In the afternoon, one keeper is on duty in the service room. Another sleeps so that he can do the night duty. The third relaxes and watches television.

3

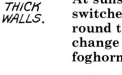

At sunset, the light must be switched on. Lens panels revolve round the light to make it flash or change colour. If it is foggy the foghorn is switched on too.

Sailors need to know which lighthouse it is that they can see. Each one has its own sequence of flashes and fog sounds, and these are marked on sailors' charts.

6

Storm waves sometimes break right over a lighthouse and make the whole building shake. The walls are specially built so that they bend but do not crack.

45

Currents and Tides

Messages in bottles are sometimes found thousands of kilometres from where they were thrown in the sea. How do they travel such a long way?

The water these people are swimming in might once have been at the North Pole. The water in the seas is moving round all the time. These pictures show you how.

1 Currents

Sailing ships used to take a long time to cross the Atlantic Ocean. Around 1780, Benjamin Franklin found that ships taking a certain route took two weeks less.

2 Franklin made a chart which showed a river of fast-flowing water in the ocean. This is called a *current*. The current Franklin found is called the Gulf Stream.

3 All the oceans have currents. They happen because warm water moves away from the equator and cooler water from the Poles flows in to take its place.

4 Scientists throw drift bottles and cards in the sea to find out about currents. Messages inside ask the finder to send them back, saying where they found them.

Tides

In most places, the sea moves regularly in over the shore and then out again. This movement is called the tide.

Scientists are not sure exactly how the tides work. But they do know that the Sun and the Moon have a pulling effect on the seas, and that this makes high and low tide. Most seashores have two high tides and two low tides every day.

This picture shows the tides which happen at the same time in different places on the Earth.

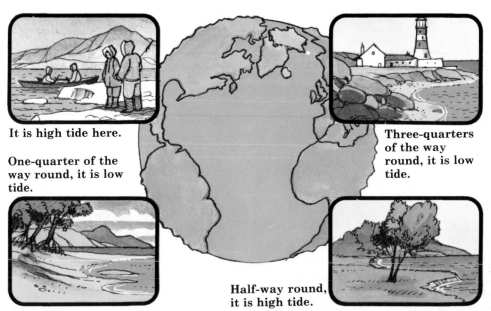

It is high tide here.

One-quarter of the way round, it is low tide.

Three-quarters of the way round, it is low tide.

Half-way round, it is high tide.

Waves and Winds

Waves

When you blow across a bowl of water, your breath ruffles the surface into little waves. The same thing happens when the wind blows across the sea.

The stronger the wind, the bigger the waves. The tallest wave ever recorded was seen in 1933 by sailors on a U.S naval ship. They saw a wave 34 metres high in the Pacific Ocean.

1 How waves move

Waves travel across the surface of the sea. You might have watched them from the seashore or from a boat. But did you know that the water itself does not travel along? The water just goes up and down as the waves pass through it. When seagulls sit on the sea, they go up and down with the water.

Winds

If you listen to a shipping forecast on the radio, you will hear that numbers are used to describe the strength of the wind.

These numbers are from a scale worked out over a hundred years ago by Admiral Beaufort. It is called the Beaufort scale, after him.

Higher numbers mean a stronger wind and so, bigger waves. Here are some of the numbers in the scale and what they mean.

Wind force 0—no wind at all.

Wind force 4—a fresh breeze.

Wind force 8—a gale is blowing.

Wind force 12 (the highest number in the scale)—means a hurricane.

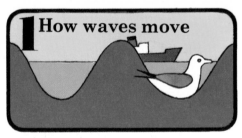

Icy Seas

If you go far enough north or south, you reach places where it is so cold that the sea freezes over. Sometimes the surface of the sea freezes into a solid sheet of ice. When it melts it breaks into pieces of *pack ice* which float on the sea.

The ice is hard, like rock, and very dangerous for ships because it floats around.

Here are some of the things you might see if you were near the North or South Pole.

Snow is packed down and changed to ice by the weight of more snow falling on top of it.

The ice slowly slides down towards the sea.

Icebergs are carried along by currents in the sea, and blown along by the wind.

Flat-topped icebergs like this one are called tabular icebergs. They are found in the sea near the South Pole.

Icebergs often make creaking noises when they move. Some small bergs are so noisy that they are called growlers.

Icebreaker ships are used to cut a passage through the ice.

Ordinary ships use the passage cut by the icebreaker. Some of them take food and supplies to scientists working near the Poles.

How icebreakers work

Icebreaker ships are specially shaped at the front so that they ride up on to the ice. Then the weight of the ship breaks the ice underneath it.

The Titanic

On a calm night in 1912, a large passenger ship called the Titanic, crashed into an iceberg in the Atlantic. It was the Titanic's first voyage and everyone thought it was unsinkable. But the iceberg tore a 30 metre hole in the side of the ship and within three hours it had sunk. About 1,500 people were drowned.

Islands

When the ice reaches the sea, huge lumps break off and become icebergs floating in the sea.

Only a little bit of an iceberg shows above the water. More than three-quarters of it is under the sea.

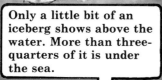

Thin, flat pieces of pack ice are formed from frozen sea water.

Islands are the tops of underwater mountains or volcanoes that stick up above the sea. Only the very tallest mountains make islands.

In 1963, a new volcano appeared in the Atlantic Ocean off Iceland. Sea volcanoes often disappear because their ash tops are washed away. But this one is still there.

The volcano cooled down to form a new island. It was named Surtsey. Now there are plants and animals on the island and people have landed there.

Some islands are made of *coral*. Coral is a hard, rock-like substance which is made by little sea animals called coral polyps. These live only in warm seas.

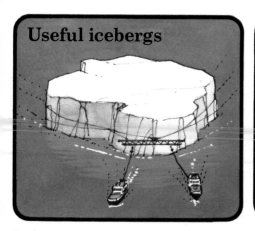

Useful icebergs

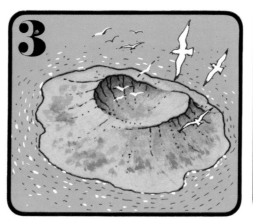

Icebergs are made of snow, so they are not salty. Some scientists think icebergs could be towed to North America and used to water the deserts.

Coral polyps attach themselves to rocks and catch food with their tentacles. They grow a chalky skeleton round themselves and this hardens to form the coral.

Over thousands of years, the coral builds up to make large reefs and islands. Rings of coral, called *atolls*, sometimes form round sunken volcanoes.

Fishing

This fisherman is on a mosaic that is nearly 2,000 years old. But we know that people were eating sea-food long before that. Sea-shells, fish bones and fish-hooks have been found in ancient rubbish tips that may be 10,000 years old.

Now fish are often caught by trawler boats. These drag enormous nets, called trawls, which scoop up the fish. Some trawlers are equipped with freezers. Some even have factory machines, which can make fish fingers and other fish products while the ship is still at sea.

Here is a fishing port which we have made up to show you how fish are caught and what happens to them afterwards.

How a fishing port works

Seabirds often follow fishing boats. They pick up any fish that are thrown overboard.

Type of fishing boat called a stern trawler. Its huge net is longer than a football pitch.

Fishing boat called a purse seiner. Its net encircles the fish and is drawn together with a rope.

Mending nets.

1 A fishing trip

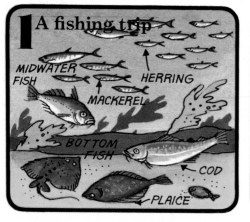

MIDWATER FISH

HERRING

MACKEREL

BOTTOM FISH

COD

PLAICE

Great numbers of these fish are caught every day. Cod and plaice are dragged up from the bottom. Herring, mackerel and tuna are caught near the surface.

Mechanical winches haul the full net up the ramp at the back of a stern trawler. On older types of ship the men have to heave the heavy nets in by hand.

The fish must be gutted or they will go bad. The crew often have to do this while standing on the wet, slippery deck of the moving ship.

Frozen fish being packed for export to other countries.

Glue factory. Fish skins and bones are used to make some kinds of glue.

Lorries delivering fresh fish to inland towns.

Grocer's shop selling canned and frozen fish, fish fingers, and margarine which is made from fish oils.

Fishmonger selling fresh fish.

Waste fish is processed in this factory. All the oil and water are squeezed out leaving a dry, grey powder called fish meal.

Fish oils are used in this factory to make soap.

Factory making ice for ships without freezers aboard.

Tractor spreading fish meal fertilizer.

Cat-food factory.

Blocks of frozen fish being unloaded from a freezer ship.

Fish-smoking factory. Kippers and other yellow fish are prepared here.

Lobster pots

Boxes of fish packed in ice.

Fish-canning factory.

Fish meal is used for feeding farm animals.

On freezer ships, the gutted fish are laid head to tail and frozen into blocks weighing 40 kg. The frozen blocks are then stored in a refrigerated hold.

Ships without freezers load up with ice before they leave port. Fish are packed in boxes with the ice. These ships must return in two weeks or the fish will go bad.

Scientists are worried that the fish in the sea will soon be used up. They are experimenting with fish farms where fish are hatched from eggs and kept in tanks.

Seaweed and Sponges

We catch and use lots of wild plants and animals from the sea. You will find out about some of them here. If we are not careful, though, we may find that we have caught them all and there are none left.

In some parts of the world there are sea farms where fish and pearls are grown. It may be possible to farm other kinds of sea-life too. Then we could be sure that we were not using it all up.

1 Did you know that ice-cream has seaweed in it? Seaweeds are used to make lots of other things too— like toothpaste, plastics, paint make-up and medicines.

2 The Japanese eat a lot of seaweed, especially a delicate red kind that grows round their shores. It is gathered like this with long hooked poles.

3 An enormous seaweed called giant kelp grows off the west coast of America. It grows extremely quickly and has been known to gain 50 centimetres in one day.

4 Giant kelp is collected by backward-moving seaweed harvester boats. Razor-sharp revolving blades slice the tops off the plants and drag them aboard.

5 The useful part of the seaweed is a gooey jelly which is made by boiling the plants. Whole seaweed is also used for animals' food and for manure.

6 Underwater farm machines may be developed in the future. Then, it might be possible to plant and look after huge fields of seaweed under the sea.

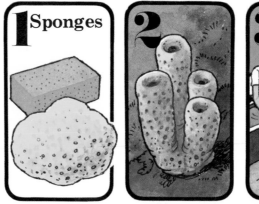

1 Sponges **2** You may have seen expensive, oddly shaped, yellow bath sponges in the shops. These are natural sponges which come from the sea.

Sponges are animals. They "breathe" water containing air and food through little holes, called pores, in their bodies. Only a few kinds are useful as bath sponges.

3 **4** Divers collect the sponges from the sea-bed. Living sponges are greyish and slimy. They are washed and stamped on or beaten to clean them.

The clean, yellow part of the sponge that we use is its skeleton. The skeletons are trimmed to make nice shapes and sent all over the world.

Pearls

1 The shells of some oysters—though not the kind of oyster people eat—contain pearls. This is very rare. Perhaps one oyster in a hundred has one.

2 Oysters are found in warm seas and people dive for them there. Skilled divers, like these Japanese women, stay down for several minutes without breathing.

3 The divers carry stones to make them sink quickly. They fill a bag with oysters and then signal to be pulled up, by tugging a rope tied round their wrists.

4 A pearl is made when a speck of grit gets inside an oyster's shell. The oyster builds up layers of pearly substance round the grit to protect itself.

5 There are pearl farms in Japan. Tiny bits of shell are put inside the oysters, which are then kept in underwater baskets for about three years.

6 The value of a pearl depends on its shape, size and colour. Occasionally, a rare black pearl is found and these are extremely valuable.

Whales

This is a blue whale. Blue whales are the biggest animals that have ever lived. Some weigh several times as much as the heaviest dinosaurs. So many whales have been hunted and killed, that now there are very few left.

Whales have tons of fat, called blubber, round their bodies to keep them warm. Whale oil is made from the blubber. People burned whale oil in lamps before electric lights were invented.

SOME BLUE WHALES WEIGH AS MUCH AS 20 ELEPHANTS.

THE SKIN MAKES A VERY SOFT LEATHER.

BLUBBER LAYER UNDER SKIN CAN BE 60cm THICK.

BLUBBER FROM ONE BLUE WHALE CAN MAKE 120 BARRELS OF OIL.

WHALE MEAT CAN BE EATEN BY PEOPLE AND ANIMALS.

A BIG WHALE MAY BE 30 METRES LONG.

Salt and Metals from the Sea

The salt which we eat with our food was once in the sea. Common salt is a *mineral* and minerals are the chemical materials rocks are made of.

There are about two cupfuls of minerals dissolved in every bucket of sea water. Most of it is common salt, which makes the sea taste salty.

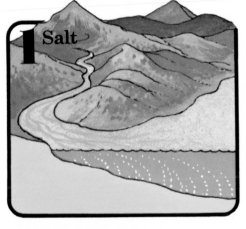

1 Salt

Rain-water and rivers wash minerals out of the rocks and into the sea. Over thousands of years, so many minerals have collected in the sea that is is now very salty.

2

Plants and animals in the sea use some of the minerals. Shellfish take calcium from the water to make their shells and seaweeds store iodine.

3

This is a salt farm which was made in China in 1971. The people are building low walls on the seashore so that they can trap shallow pools of sea water.

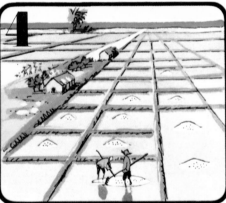

4

The sea water evaporates and so the pools dry up. The salt which was in the water is left behind as tiny, white crystals. Then it is collected and cleaned.

Metals in the sea

Mining the minerals from the sea is more difficult than on land. Scientists have invented deep-sea bulldozers and pipes to suck the minerals to the surface.

THERE IS GOLD IN THE WATER, BUT IT COSTS TOO MUCH TO COLLECT IT.

DIAMONDS ARE COLLECTED FROM THE MUD AT THE BOTTOM.

LUMPS OF MANGANESE AND COBALT ARE SUCKED UP FROM THE SEA FLOOR.

Making fresh water

SALTY SEA WATER

FRESH WATER IS PIPED AWAY.

Some hot, dry countries have factories where the salt is taken out of sea water to make fresh water. This is called *desalination*.

When sea water evaporates, tiny droplets of fresh water leave its surface, and the salt stays behind. This fresh water is collected and piped away.

Oil under the Sea

In rocks deep under the sea, there are tiny drops of oil. To reach the oil a hole is drilled from a drilling rig right down into the sea-bed.

Scientists think oil is probably made from the bodies of tiny sea creatures which lived millions of years ago. When the creatures died they were buried by mud and sand, and slowly they changed into little drops of oil.

Over millions of years, thick layers of mud have settled at the bottom of the sea and hardened to form layers of rock on top of the oil.

This is the derrick which supports the drilling pipes.

The crew are brought to the rig by helicopter. Usually they stay on the rig for 14 days and then go ashore for 14 days. About a hundred men live on the rig.

Underwater divers check the anchors and drilling pipes to make sure they are secure. The rig has to be held very firmly in position, especially when the sea is rough.

These workers are called roughnecks. Here they are adding another pipe to the drill so they can bore deeper into the rocks of the sea-bed.

DIAMONDS

The drilling bits have to be very strong to cut through the rocks. They are made of specially strengthened steel and some are studded with diamonds.

Exploring the Sea-bed

When you are standing on the seashore, or sailing in a boat, it is hard to imagine what goes on in the depths below. Until about a hundred years ago, people thought the sea-bed was completely flat and smooth.

Scientists have now discovered deep valleys and towering mountains under the sea. Some parts of the ocean are so deep that Mount Everest, which is 8,848 m high, would fit under the sea without appearing above the surface.

Diving saucers

People who explore under the sea are called *aquanauts*. They travel in vehicles like this diving saucer. It has a mechanical claw to pick up rocks from the sea-bed.

A bottle dropped in the ocean would be broken by the weight of the water before it reached the bottom. Diving saucers are strongly built to bear this weight.

1 Land under the sea

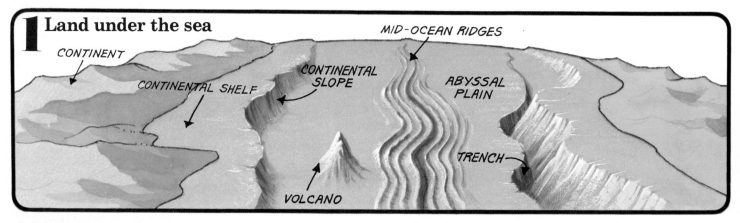

MID-OCEAN RIDGES

CONTINENT

CONTINENTAL SHELF

CONTINENTAL SLOPE

ABYSSAL PLAIN

TRENCH

VOLCANO

The large bits of land which stick up out of the sea are called *continents*. Round the continents the sea-bed is shallow and is called the *continental shelf*.

At the edge of the continental shelf the sea-bed dips down steeply to the *abyssal plain*. There are ridges of high mountains in the middle of the ocean.

In some oceans there are deep valleys called *trenches* in the sea-bed. The deepest place in the ocean is the Mariana trench, 11,033 m down in the Pacific.

2

CONTINENTAL SHELF

CONTINENTAL SLOPE

ABYSSAL PLAIN

Near the land, the bottom of the sea is coated with a thick layer of mud called *sediment*. The sediment is carried into the sea by rivers and the wind.

The mud spills over the edge of the continental shelf like a waterfall over a cliff. It carves a valley in the sea-bed and then flows out over the abyssal plain.

3

In the deep ocean, there is a layer of sediment called *ooze*. This is made of the remains of dead fish and sea plants which fall to the bottom of the sea.

Echo-sounding

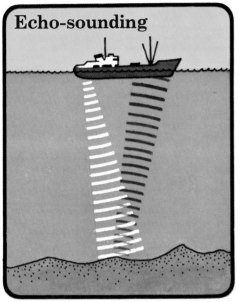

Scientists measure the depth of the ocean by making echos. They time how long a sound takes to echo back from the sea-bed.

Sound moves about 1,500 metres a second through water. So they can work out how deep the water is from how many seconds the echo takes.

Sea-bed rocks

Samples of rock are dug out of the sea-bed with a corer. Scientists study them to learn more about our planet. The corer is a long tube with a 1,000 kg weight on top. It is dropped into the sea and the weight forces the tube into the sea-bed. Then the corer is hauled up with the tube full of rock.

1 The deepest dive

On 23 January, 1960, Jacques Piccard and Don Walsh planned to descend to the deepest part of the deepest ocean in the world.

Their diving craft was called Trieste. In it they hoped to reach the bottom of Mariana Trench, 11,033 m down in the Pacific.

Trieste was a bathyscaph, which is a small, ball-shaped room joined to huge tanks to keep it afloat. The tanks are filled with petrol.

The two men squashed into the tiny room. The walls were made of strong steel to bear the weight of the water deep in the ocean.

When they let out some of the petrol, Trieste began to go down. They sank through the water at a speed of a metre a second.

At 400 metres it grew dark, for hardly any sunlight filters this deep. They switched on the spotlight and saw coloured fish.

After four hours, they reckoned they were near the bottom. To slow down, they made Trieste lighter by throwing out lead weights.

A cloud of mud billowed round them as they landed, and then they saw a fish swimming in the sea at the bottom of the world.

Divers

Until about a hundred years ago, people could stay under water for only as long as they could hold their breath. Then the first diving suits were made. The diver wore a big helmet and air was pumped into the helmet through a pipe. The diver had to be very careful not to get his air pipe twisted.

Now, people can swim under water almost as freely as fish. They carry their own air in a piece of apparatus called an *aqualung*. This was invented about 30 years ago.

1 Aqualunging

An aqualung diver straps cannisters of air on his back and breathes the air through a mouthpiece. There is usually enough air for an hour's swim.

2

There is plenty of work under the sea for aqualung divers. They check underwater oil wells and pipelines, build bridges and study sea life and the sea-bed.

3

Divers use special waterproof cameras to take pictures of sea animals and the land under the sea. They need to use flashlights in the dull, underwater light.

4

Wet suits keep divers warm in the water. The rubber suit traps a film of water next to the skin. The diver's body heats this water which in turn keeps him warm.

5

After diving below 15 metres, divers have to come up very slowly. Otherwise they get agonising pains and jerks called the bends in their knees and elbows.

6

Aqualung divers do not usually go deeper than about 100 metres. Below this, divers wear thick helmets and suits so that they are not crushed by the weight of water.

7

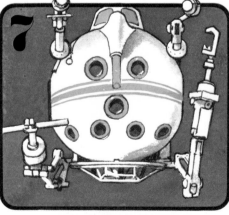

This is Beaver IV. It can go much deeper in the sea than a diver. With its movable arms it can work on oil wells and pipelines 600 metres below the surface.

Finding treasure

One day, when he was diving for sponges, a young Greek boy found these statues. They sank with a ship and lay at the bottom of the sea for over 2,000 years.

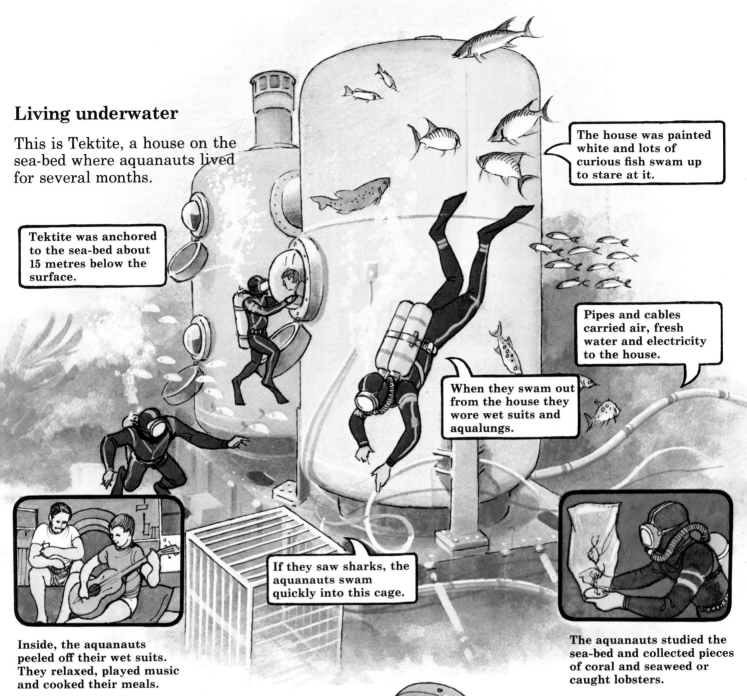

Living underwater

This is Tektite, a house on the sea-bed where aquanauts lived for several months.

Tektite was anchored to the sea-bed about 15 metres below the surface.

The house was painted white and lots of curious fish swam up to stare at it.

Pipes and cables carried air, fresh water and electricity to the house.

When they swam out from the house they wore wet suits and aqualungs.

If they saw sharks, the aquanauts swam quickly into this cage.

Inside, the aquanauts peeled off their wet suits. They relaxed, played music and cooked their meals.

The aquanauts studied the sea-bed and collected pieces of coral and seaweed or caught lobsters.

Treasure hunters dream of finding chests of gold, silver or jewels in shipwrecks. Now, divers wearing aqualungs can stay underwater long enough to search the wrecks.

Salty sea water eats away wood and metal so the divers have to raise their treasure very gently. One way is to use an air balloon which floats up slowly through the water.

This is the Swedish warship Vasa. It lay on the sea-bed for over 300 years until it was raised and put in a museum. Sea chests, cannons and even a felt hat were found inside.

Animals of the Sea

Imagine you could dive right to the bottom of the ocean. At first you swim through warm, sunlit waters. Then you enter a cold, blue-green coloured place. As you sink lower, it becomes pitch black and the water is freezing cold.

There are no plants down here because plants need sunlight to grow. Deep-sea animals eat each other and dead creatures that drift down from above.

Here is some of the wildlife you might meet on your trip to the bottom of the ocean.

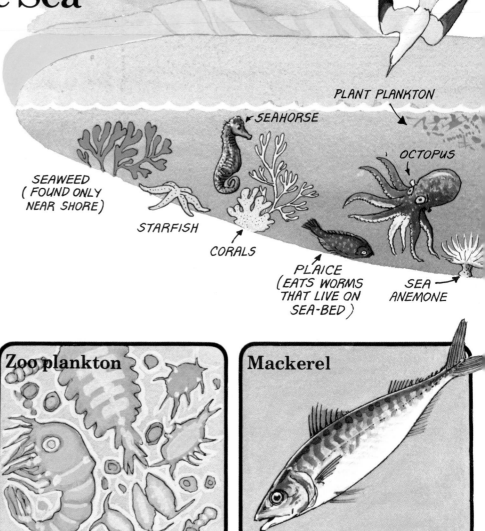

FISH-EATING SEABIRD

PLANT PLANKTON

SEAHORSE

OCTOPUS

SEAWEED (FOUND ONLY NEAR SHORE)

STARFISH

CORALS

PLAICE (EATS WORMS THAT LIVE ON SEA-BED)

SEA ANEMONE

Plant plankton

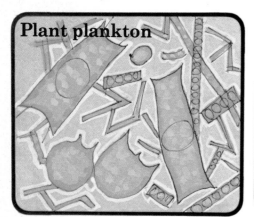

Millions of tiny plants, called *plant plankton*, live near the surface. This is what they look like under a microscope. Really they are smaller than a fullstop.

Zoo plankton

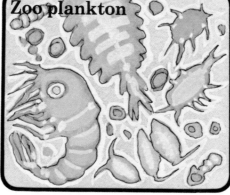

Zoo plankton are tiny animals that feed on plant plankton. Some are the babies of larger animals. Most zooplankton are about the size of the letters on this page.

Mackerel

These fish live near the surface and eat zooplankton. They have dark skin on top and silvery skin underneath so that their enemies cannot see them too easily.

Lantern fish

Fish in the dim blue-green waters have very good eyesight. Some have lights on their bodies made by chemicals inside them. These are to confuse their enemies.

Viper fish

Food is scarce in the dark depths. Fish here have huge mouths and expanding stomachs so they can eat anything that comes their way.

Deep-sea angler fish

The deep-sea angler fish has a "fishing rod" with a light to attract fish into its gaping mouth. It is too slow and blind to chase its food.

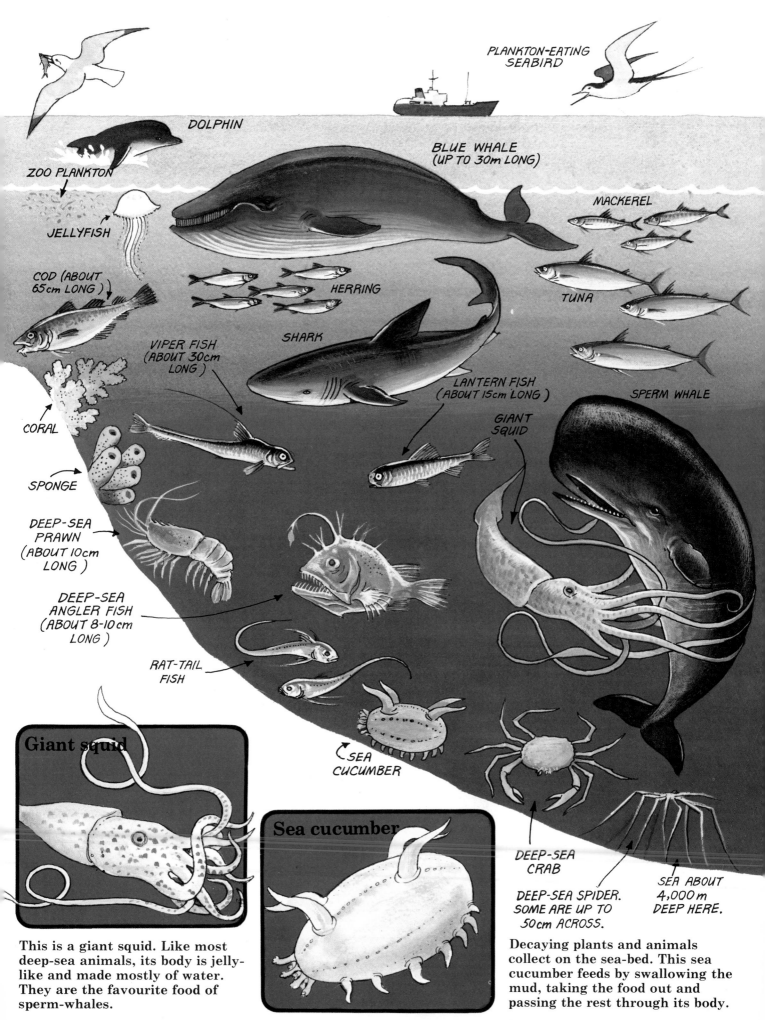

PLANKTON-EATING SEABIRD

DOLPHIN

ZOO PLANKTON

JELLYFISH

BLUE WHALE
(UP TO 30m LONG)

MACKEREL

COD (ABOUT
65cm LONG)

HERRING

TUNA

VIPER FISH
(ABOUT 30cm
LONG)

SHARK

LANTERN FISH
(ABOUT 15cm LONG)

SPERM WHALE

CORAL

GIANT
SQUID

SPONGE

DEEP-SEA
PRAWN
(ABOUT 10cm
LONG)

DEEP-SEA
ANGLER FISH
(ABOUT 8-10cm
LONG)

RAT-TAIL
FISH

SEA
CUCUMBER

DEEP-SEA
CRAB

DEEP-SEA SPIDER.
SOME ARE UP TO
50cm ACROSS.

SEA ABOUT
4,000 m
DEEP HERE.

Giant squid

This is a giant squid. Like most deep-sea animals, its body is jelly-like and made mostly of water. They are the favourite food of sperm-whales.

Sea cucumber

Decaying plants and animals collect on the sea-bed. This sea cucumber feeds by swallowing the mud, taking the food out and passing the rest through its body.

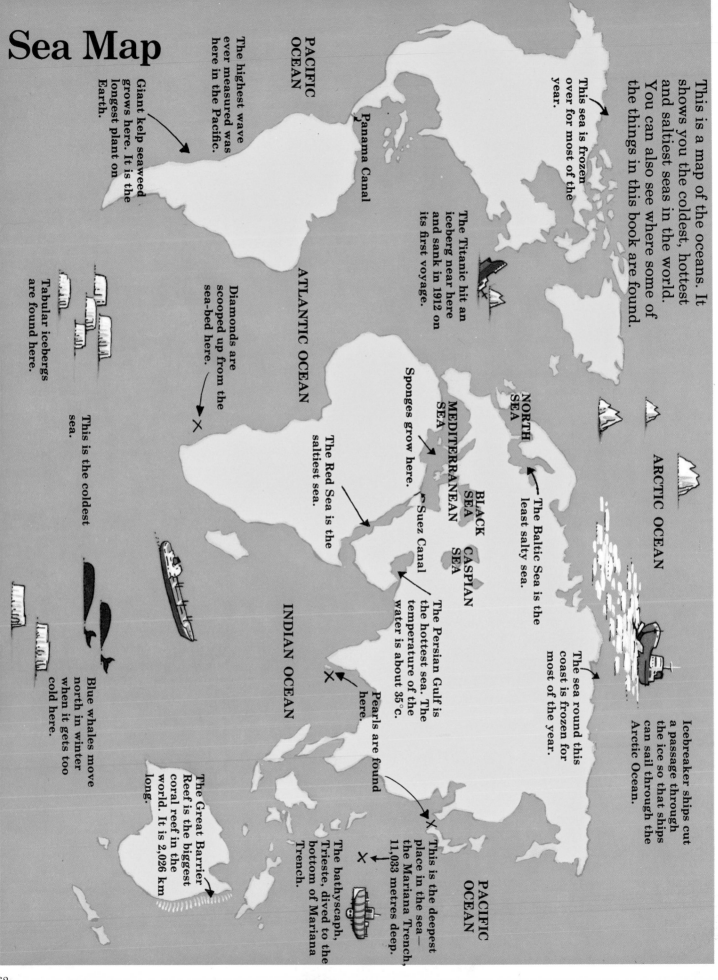

Sea Map

This is a map of the oceans. It shows you the coldest, hottest and saltiest seas in the world. You can also see where some of the things in this book are found.

This sea is frozen over for most of the year.

The Titanic hit an iceberg near here and sank in 1912 on its first voyage.

PACIFIC OCEAN

Panama Canal

The highest wave ever measured was here in the Pacific.

Giant kelp seaweed grows here. It is the longest plant on Earth.

Tabular icebergs are found here.

Diamonds are scooped up from the sea-bed here.

ATLANTIC OCEAN

This is the coldest sea.

Blue whales move north in winter when it gets too cold here.

Sponges grow here.

MEDITERRANEAN SEA

The Red Sea is the saltiest sea.

Suez Canal

BLACK SEA

CASPIAN SEA

NORTH SEA

The Baltic Sea is the least salty sea.

ARCTIC OCEAN

The sea round this coast is frozen for most of the year.

Icebreaker ships cut a passage through the ice so that ships can sail through the Arctic Ocean.

The Persian Gulf is the hottest sea. The temperature of the water is about 35°c.

Pearls are found here.

INDIAN OCEAN

The Great Barrier Reef is the biggest coral reef in the world. It is 2,026 km long.

This is the deepest place in the sea — the Mariana Trench, 11,033 metres deep.

The bathyscaph, Trieste, dived to the bottom of Mariana Trench.

PACIFIC OCEAN

Sea Words

Abyssal plain
Vast flat area at the bottom of an ocean.

Aqualung
Cylinders of air used by divers so they can breathe under water.

Aquanaut
Person who explores under the sea.

Atoll
Ring of coral, making an island.

Bathyscaph
Underwater vehicle for deep sea exploration.

Buoys
Floating markers in the sea showing dangerous spots and safe channels.

Continental shelf
The shallow sea-bed round the edge of a large piece of land.

Coral
Rock-like substance made by little sea animals called coral polyps.

Cove
Horse-shoe shaped coastline made where there is soft rock behind a ridge of hard rock.

Current
River of water flowing through the ocean.

Desalination
The process by which fresh water is made from sea water.

Dock
Deep basin in a port in which the water is always kept at the same level.

Evaporation
Water changing into tiny invisible droplets, called water vapour, in the air.

Groyne
Wall to stop sand or pebbles being pushed sideways along a beach.

Iceberg
Huge lump of ice which breaks away from ice-covered land and floats in the sea.

Island
The top of an underwater mountain or volcano which sticks up above the sea.

Lock
A place where boats can be moved from one water level to another.

Longshore drift
The movement of sand or pebbles sideways along a beach by waves.

Ooze
Mud-like substance at the bottom of the sea made of decaying plants and animals.

Pack ice
Pieces of frozen sea water floating on the sea.

Pebble
Small piece of rock made smooth and rounded by constant rubbing against other rocks in the sea.

Plankton
Tiny plants and animals that live near the surface of the sea.

Port
The side of the boat that is to your left when you stand on deck facing the front.

Radar
Radio waves sent out by ships and reflected back to them by land and other ships, to help them see their way.

Sand
Little pieces of sea-shell and very hard rock.

Sea level
The level of the sea, used as a standard for measuring heights and depths of land.

Shore
The place where the sea washes against the land.

Sonar
Sound waves sent down by ships and reflected back by the sea-bed. They show how deep the sea is.

Spit
Sand bank joined on to the land at one end.

Stack
Pillar of rock, separated from a headland when the rock in between wears away.

Starboard
The side of a boat that is to your right when you are standing on deck and facing the front.

Tide
Regular movement of the sea up and down the shore.

Trawler
Type of fishing boat which drags a net.

Trench
Very deep part of the ocean.

Wave
Ridge of water in the sea.

Ship Spotter's Guide

When a ship is at sea, all you can see is its shape outlined against the sky. The main kinds of ships are quite easy to identify from their shape.

Here are some pictures of ships that you might see in a port, at sea or perhaps on television.

Passenger ships

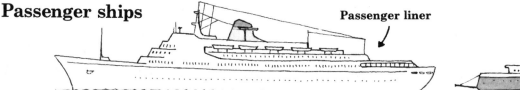

Passenger liner

These carry people on journeys and cruises. They have a high superstructure which is the part of a ship above the main deck.

This has several decks, one on top of the other, big funnels and lots of portholes for the cabins. Length about 150–320 m.

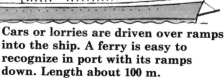

Car ferry

Cars or lorries are driven over ramps into the ship. A ferry is easy to recognize in port with its ramps down. Length about 100 m.

Train ferry

Hovercraft

Hydrofoil

This has railway lines inside and trains are driven in the back. Quite a wide boat with several decks. Length about 100 m.

This skims along just above the water. At sea, its "skirt" is puffed up with air. In port, the air is let out. About 30 m long.

A hydrofoil has wings underneath called foils. The craft speeds across the water on its foils. Length about 30 m.

Cargo ships

Tanker

General cargo ship

The deck is usually flat and the crew's cabins and bridge are in a small superstructure near the back of the ship.

Long, low ship with flat deck. Pipes and pumping gear on deck and a catwalk for crew to walk along. Some tankers are about 300 m long.

Carries cargo of all shapes and sizes. Has a superstructure near the back and usually has lots of cranes on deck. About 150 m long.

Short-sea trader

Container ship

Fishing boat

Stern trawler

Small ship which carries cargo such as grain, fruit or coal on short voyages. Has cranes and pulleys to lift the cargo. Length about 80 m.

Cargo is carried in boxes called containers. These are stacked on top of each other in the hold. Length about 280 m.

Fishing boat with opening in the back, or stern, to haul the nets through. Two tall masts to hold the nets. Length about 40 m.

Naval ships

Aircraft carrier

Destroyer

These are usually painted grey. They have guns on deck and lots of aerials and scanners for radar and radio.

The deck is flat and empty for planes to use as a runway. There is a small superstructure on one side of the deck. About 250 m long.

Fast ship with lots of guns, missiles and torpedo weapons. Some have a helicopter deck and radar dome. About 150 m long.

Harbour boats

Submarine

Pilot launch

Tug (Towboat)

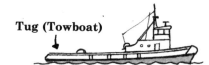

This is long and pen-shaped with small superstructure on top. On nuclear-powered submarines, the superstructure is near the front. Length 80–130 m.

Small, fast motor launch which carries a trained pilot out to a ship. The pilot then steers the ship into harbour.

Pushes and pulls the ships into place in the harbour. It is lower at the back than at the front and some have bumpers for pushing.

Part Three
Peoples of the World

What you will find in this part of the book.

Peoples and their countries

There are over 150 countries in the world. Some of them are huge, with hundreds of millions of people, while others are as small as cities with populations of only a few thousand.

People in different countries have their own customs, traditions, languages and beliefs. Some of the large countries have lots of different peoples, each with their own customs and languages.

1 What is a country?

Each country has its government which rules the people. This picture shows Capitol Hill in Washington, U.S.A. where the American Government, called the Congress, meets.

2

Every country has a flag and most have a national anthem. The Union Jack, seen here on the Tower of London, is the flag of the United Kingdom.

3

Countries have their own money and stamps which can usually be used only within their boundaries. Coins, notes and stamps often have pictures of famous people or places on them.

4

People in different countries usually speak different languages. In some countries, several languages are spoken and used on signposts like this one in the Sahara Desert in Mali.

5

In Japan, it is a custom for people to greet each other by bowing. People in other countries have their own special customs too, such as shaking hands.

Travelling abroad

To travel to another country you need a travel document called a passport. This shows your nationality, and the country you come from.

You need special permission to enter some countries. In these cases, you must have a visa stamped in your passport by the country's embassy.

At the boundaries between countries there are barriers across the roads. Here the frontier police examine your passport and watch out for smugglers.

Before you can buy anything in another country, you have to get your money changed at a bank or *bureau de change*.

Flags

The red maple tree leaf on the Canadian flag is the symbol of Canada. This flag was first used in 1965.

The Union Jack, flag of the United Kingdom, is a combination of the red cross of St George, white cross of St Andrew and red cross of St Patrick.

The Australian flag shows the Southern Cross, a group of stars which can be seen in the Australian sky.

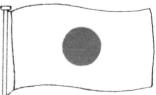

The red circle on the Japanese flag represents the sun and the name Japan means "land of the rising sun" in Japanese.

The hammer of the factory worker and the sickle of the farm worker appear on the flag of the U.S.S.R., which was first used in 1917.

The flag of the U.S.A. has 50 stars, one for each of the states. The 13 stripes represent the 13 original states.

On the flag of Saudi Arabia are the words "There is no god but God and Muhammad is his Prophet", written in Arabic.

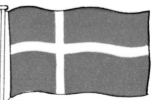

The Danish flag is the oldest in the world. It has been used for over 600 years.

Tribal peoples

In some parts of the world there are groups, or tribes of people whose customs and traditions are different from those of the country they live in. These peoples often have their own leaders, but they still have to obey the laws of the country they live in. Nowadays many of these people are moving to live in towns and are giving up their traditional ways of life.

The Bedouin are a people who live by herding camels and sheep in the Arabian desert. Nowadays, many of them are settling to live in the towns.

The Masai live in Kenya and Tanzania, in East Africa. They have their own language and live mainly by herding cattle.

Many different tribal peoples live in the Xingu National Park, a reservation in the Amazon forest, in South America.

Rich and poor countries

The rich countries are those which have lots of factories or large quantities of a natural product such as oil. Countries where most people work in factories or offices are called industrialized countries.

In the poorer countries most people still work on the land as farmers. They do not have many factories and often grow crops such as sugar, coffee or cotton to sell to the rich countries.

Country collections

There are lots of ways of making a country collection. You could collect everything you can find about one country, such as fruit and food wrappers, coins, stamps, postcards and pictures from travel brochures. Or you could limit your collection to one topic, such as stamps, or pictures of national costumes, flags or football players and collect these for lots of different countries.

Peoples' ancestors

Many millions of years ago, our ancestors were monkey-like creatures living in the trees. Like all other animals, people have slowly developed and changed to become as they are today.

Everyone in the world belongs to the same biological group, or species. This group is called *Homo sapiens*, which is Latin for "wise man".

These monkey-like creatures lived about 14 million years ago and are the ancestors of people. There were no people on Earth then.

The first people lived about three million years ago. They ate grubs and berries and hunted for animals which they killed with rocks and sticks.

Gradually, our early ancestors learned how to hunt larger animals. They made tools for cutting meat by chipping stones to give them sharp edges.

Tent made of animal skins.

People first discovered they could grow food by planting seeds about 11,000 years ago. They settled near their farmland and built villages.

The villages gradually grew into towns. People learned how to weave and make pottery and traded things they made with people from other towns.

For hundreds of thousands of years, people lived by hunting animals and collecting fruits to eat. There were no towns or villages and they lived in caves, or in huts built from sticks and animal skins or grass.

Chipping a rock to make a stone tool.

They were skilled at making sharp tools from stones, or from the bones or antlers of animals. They had not yet discovered how to weave cloth or to sew and their clothes were made from animal skins.

68

Races of people

There are four main races of people living in the world today, though all of them belong to the same group, or species of mankind: *Homo sapiens*.

Each race has its own special characteristics, such as the narrow eyes of the Mongoloid race, or the black skin of Negroes. Scientists think that early people in different parts of the world gradually developed characteristics that helped them to survive.

This Chinese boy belongs to the Mongoloid race.

Aboriginal boy from Australia belongs to the Australoid race.

This man from South Africa belongs to the Negroid race.

This Swiss girl belongs to the Caucasoid race.

Black skin protects people from the sun in very hot, wet places and the narrow eyes of Mongoloid people are a protection against extreme cold. Today racial differences are less important, because clothes, houses, heating and prepared foods enable people of any race to survive almost anywhere.

Tools

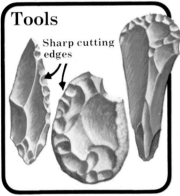

Sharp cutting edges

People first learned how to make stone tools about 2½ million years ago. Later as they became more skilful they made sharp stone scrapers and knives.

Metals

Blowing on fire to make it hotter.

Metal tools were first made over 5,000 years ago. They lasted longer and were easier to make than stone tools. Copper and gold were used first.

Cooking

Cooking was probably learned by accident when meat fell into the fire. It made it tastier and easier to chew. People roasted food on hot stones.

Clothes

Bone needles were invented 40,000 years ago. They were used for sewing skins together with leather strips, and for decorating them with shells and teeth.

Beliefs

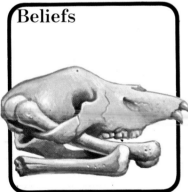

This cave bear's skull with a leg bone through it was found in a cave where early people lived. They probably believed it would make magic.

Painting

People discovered how to paint with powdered coloured rocks, mixed with animal fat. Their brushes were made of animal hair.

Pottery

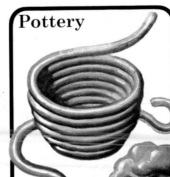

The Stone Age farmers were the first people to discover how to make pottery by baking clay in a fire. They made pots from coils of clay.

Writing

The marks on this piece of clay are some of the first writing. It was done by people called the Sumerians who lived about 5,000 years ago.

Language and writing

Over 4,000 languages are spoken in the world today. In some countries there are several languages and in India there are over 800. Sometimes people in one country speak different versions, or dialects of the same language. Some languages, such as English and Spanish, are spoken in many different parts of the world*.

Here are six children from different countries speaking in their own languages.

Hej, jag heter, Margareta.

This is Swedish. It is pronounced "Hay, yag heer-ta Mar-gar-ret-a" and means "Hello, my name is Margareta".

Hola, me llamo Pablo.

This is Spanish. It is pronounced "O-la, may ya-mo Pablo" and means "Hello, my name is Pablo".

ЗДРАВСТВУЙТЕ, МЕНЯ ЗОВУТ САША

This is Russian. It is pronounced "Is-drast-vooey-ti-ey men-yah zov-wot Sarsha" and means "Hello, my name is Sarsha"

Language families

People who study languages have discovered that many of them are related and can be grouped together into language families. This chart shows some of the languages in the Indo-European family. There are eight main groups in this language family. Two of the groups: Germanic and Romance, and some of the languages in them, are shown here.

INDO-EUROPEAN LANGUAGE FAMILY About half the world's peoples speak a language from this family.	GERMANIC The languages in this group developed from a language spoken long ago.	GERMAN	GUTEN MORGEN
		ENGLISH	GOOD MORNING
		DUTCH	GOEDE MORGEN
		SWEDISH	GOD MORGON
		NORWEGIAN	GOD MORGEN
	ROMANCE The languages in this group all developed from Latin. The words shown here mean "man" in English.	ITALIAN	UOMO
		SPANISH	HOMBRE
		FRENCH	HOMME
		PORTUGUESE	HOMEM
		ROMANIAN	OM

All the languages in a family developed from the same parent language. As groups of people spread out across the world, they took their language with them. They began to pronounce words in a slightly different way from their ancestors, and had to find new words for foreign things, so gradually their language changed.

Writing

An alphabet is a set of symbols which stand for the sounds which make words. There are many different alphabets and ways of writing. Arabic is written from right to left, and Chinese does not have an alphabet at all. Instead it uses "characters" to stand for words or parts of words.

1 — Latin or Roman alphabet

A B C D E
F G H I J K
L M N O P
Q R S T U
V W X Y Z

Most West European languages use this alphabet. Some of them add signs to the letters, e.g. ö, to show how they should be pronounced.

2 — Arabic alphabet

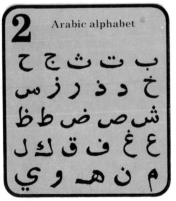

Arabic is the second most widely used alphabet. Other languages such as Persian and Urdu (used in Pakistan) are also written in it.

3 — Picture signs / Modern Chinese characters

Man · Tree · Bird

Modern Chinese characters developed from picture signs. They are now written from left to right, but used to be written in columns down the page.

This is Arabic. It is pronounced "Mar-huba, iss-mee Layla" and means "Hello, my name is Layla".

This is Hindi which is spoken in India. It is pronounced "Nam-as-tay, mera naam Rah-day Shaam hi" and means "Hello, my name is Rahday Shaam".

This is Chinese. It is pronounced "Nee how, wah ming tzer Tsee-ow Hoong" and means "Hello, my name is Tseeow Hoong".

Numbers

European	Arab	Chinese
1	١	一
2	٢	二
3	٣	三
4	٤	四
5	٥	五

The numbers used in western Europe are called Arabic numerals and developed from numbers used by the Arabs 1,000 years ago. Chinese and some other languages have their own signs for numbers.

Greek

Greek was the first European language to have a written form. The word "alphabet" comes from the names of the first two Greek letters: *alpha* and *beta*.

African languages

This man is reading a newspaper written in Swahili, the main East African language. Over 1,000 languages are spoken in Africa. Some have no written form.

India

Hindi, which this girl is learning to read, is one of the languages of India. Many Indians speak Hindustani, a mixture of Hindi and another language called Urdu.

South America

PORTUGUESE
SPANISH
AMERICAN INDIAN

Many South American countries used to be ruled by Spain or Portugal, so Spanish and Portuguese are spoken there. American Indian languages are also spoken.

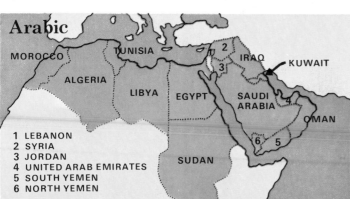

Arabic

MOROCCO
TUNISIA
ALGERIA
LIBYA
EGYPT
IRAQ
KUWAIT
SAUDI ARABIA
OMAN
SUDAN

1 LEBANON
2 SYRIA
3 JORDAN
4 UNITED ARAB EMIRATES
5 SOUTH YEMEN
6 NORTH YEMEN

Arabic is the official language of all these countries. It spread out across these areas long ago, when followers of the Prophet Muhammad converted the people to their religion, Islam. The Islamic holy book, the Koran, is written in Arabic.

Chinese

There are lots of Chinese dialects, but everyone can understand these posters as they all use the same written language. The main dialect is Mandarin.

Written Chinese has over 40,000 different characters. Children at school need learn only about 3,000 of them for everyday use.

Money

Each country has its own money called its currency.*Some have the same name for their currency—more than 20 countries use "dollars"—but they all have different values.

The foreign exchange rate decides how much of another country's currency you can buy with your money. This rate often varies from day to day.

Notes and coins

▲ Indian 100 rupee note. Writing is in eight Indian languages and English.

Greek 50 drachma note which shows the head of Helen of Troy, daughter of an ancient Greek god.

2 drachma piece

Spanish 100 peseta note with picture of a Spanish composer. ▼

▲ Iranian 50 rial note and 5 and 10 rial coins. Note shows ancient temple of Shiraz and antelope, old symbol of Iran.

1 Shops and shopping

This is a market called a *souk* in Jerusalem. There are no fixed prices and the stallkeeper and shopper argue about how much the goods are worth until they can agree a price.

2 In shops like this French greengrocer's the prices are fixed and shoppers do not usually bargain for a lower price.

4 This is an open-air market in Peru. Women bring food they have grown, but do not need, to sell to other villagers.

*The chart on pages 92-95 shows what each country's currency is.

72

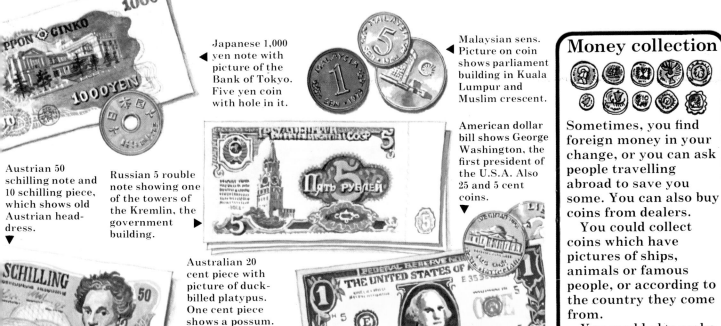

Japanese 1,000 yen note with picture of the Bank of Tokyo. Five yen coin with hole in it.

Malaysian sens. Picture on coin shows parliament building in Kuala Lumpur and Muslim crescent.

American dollar bill shows George Washington, the first president of the U.S.A. Also 25 and 5 cent coins.

Austrian 50 schilling note and 10 schilling piece, which shows old Austrian head-dress.

Russian 5 rouble note showing one of the towers of the Kremlin, the government building.

Australian 20 cent piece with picture of duck-billed platypus. One cent piece shows a possum.

Money collection

Sometimes, you find foreign money in your change, or you can ask people travelling abroad to save you some. You can also buy coins from dealers.

You could collect coins which have pictures of ships, animals or famous people, or according to the country they come from.

You could also make a collection of your own country's money, looking out for old or unusual coins.

3 Most big cities in the world have supermarkets which sell tinned and packaged foods. In America they stay open late nearly every night.

Living without money

Bushmen, who live in the Kalahari desert in Africa, use very little money. They hunt animals for food, build their own houses and make clothes from animal skins. Some are now beginning to work on farms for wages.

These people live and work on an Israeli kibbutz. They are given food and houses, and a little money for luxuries.

5 These women in a village in Iran are swopping a sack of grain for a carpet they have woven. Exchanging things like this is called bartering.

Money changers

This shopkeeper in Oman earns his living by buying and selling foreign currencies to tradesmen and travellers.

Storing wealth

The heavy gold earrings worn by this young Fulani girl from Africa, are her family's wealth. If they need money, they will sell some of the gold.

Unusual money

In this desert market in Ethiopia, people are paying for the things they need with bars of salt, which they use like money.

Food and cooking

In many countries, people eat very little meat. They have one main kind of filling food and eat it with sauces made with vegetables, spices or herbs. In Asia and the Middle East, the filling food is rice, in Africa it is maize, millet or white vegetables called yams. Potatoes are eaten in Europe and also in South America where they first came from. Everywhere people use flour made from wheat or other kinds of grain to make bread.

China

This family is eating steamed rice or noodles with vegetables and eggs or fish. Sometimes they flavour it with soya bean sauce. The Chinese do not eat much meat.

India

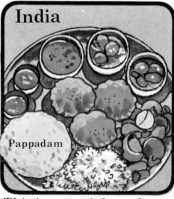

Pappadam

This is a special meal from western India. In the little bowls are rice, lentils, vegetable curry and crisps called pappadams. The curry is spicy but not always hot.

West Africa

Kitchen where food is cooked over a fire.

Millet

Forbidden foods

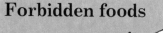

Some people do not eat certain foods because their religions forbid them. Hindus will not eat beef as cows are thought to be sacred and some do not eat any meat, fish or eggs as they are not supposed to kill animals. Muslims think pigs are unclean and do not eat pork. Jews have many rules and the foods which they may eat are called "kosher" foods.

Italy

This is a spaghetti-making machine. Spaghetti is a type of pasta made from wheat flour. It is cooked in different ways with meat, tomatoes, cheese or fish.

Germany

Many different kinds of sausages and smoked meats are eaten with warm, filling soups, pickled vegetables and rye bread called pumpernickel.

Cooking

In many parts of the world, outside the cities, people do not have gas or electric stoves. They cook over open fires or in clay ovens.

Cooking makes some foods tastier and easier to chew and digest. It also kills germs in the food. Cooked food usually keeps longer without going bad.

1 Before she can start cooking, this Indian woman has to light a wood fire. She cooks the food in shallow metal pans over the fire.

2 Women in a village in Cyprus share this clay oven for baking bread and pies. Most have stoves at home, but no ovens.

3 People who live in tents often barbeque their food on sticks. They have few pans to pack when they move camp.

Tall tower called a granary where grain is stored to keep it dry and away from rats.

Women work with their babies strapped to their backs.

Bowl made from dried skin of a fruit called a gourd.

In many African countries people grow a grain called millet. These village women from Upper Volta are pounding it to make a coarse flour.

They make a kind of porridge from the millet flour and eat it with vegetables and a peppery sauce. Meat is eaten only on special occasions.

Tunisia

This Tunisian family are eating a bowl of couscous. This is coarsely ground wheat, boiled and eaten with a vegetable or meat sauce.

Peru

This woman is making special pancakes, called tortillas, and filling them with potato spiced with hot peppers and lemon for her family's lunch.

Milk and cheese

1 This is a dairy in Denmark. Huge herds of cows are milked quickly by machines to supply city people with milk.

2 People use the milk of lots of different animals such as sheep, goats, llamas and camels. This woman is milking a yak.

3 Milk keeps much longer if it is made into butter, cheese or yoghurt. This Bedouin woman is making butter in a goatskin.

4 These Swiss cheese makers are draining the "whey" from the solid milk "curds" which will be put in a mould to make a cheese called Emmental.

Gruyère from Switzerland

Brie from France

Manchego from Spain

Feta from Greece

Edam from Holland

Stilton from England

These are some cheeses from countries in Europe.

The hungry world

Half the people in the world do not have enough to eat and millions die every year from starvation. Floods and droughts, poverty and wars prevent people in the developing countries from getting enough to eat. In richer countries people suffer diseases caused by eating too much rich or processed food.

Recipe for an Indian drink

To make this Indian drink, called *lassi*, you need a pot of plain yogurt, cold water, sugar, vanilla essence and a screw-topped container.

Put the yogurt into the container, then fill the yogurt pot with cold water and pour it in too. Add a teaspoonful of sugar and about 3 drops of vanilla essence. Screw on the top of the container and shake the mixture well. It tastes best chilled or with ice.

To make strawberry *lassi*, use strawberry flavoured yogurt and leave out the sugar and vanilla. You could use other flavours of yogurt too.

75

Clothes

Traditional clothes are still worn in many parts of the world. These clothes are suited to the climate and do not change with fashion. Loose, flowing clothes, such as saris and sarongs, are cool to wear. Thick layers of fur or padded felt clothes help keep people warm. It is usually the women who still dress in the traditional way. Men and young people, especially in cities, are now buying western-styled clothes.

1 Clothes for hot countries

Saris, which are worn by Indian women, are 6m lengths of silk or cotton cloth. Under their saris, they wear petticoats and short blouses.

2

Men and women in South-East Asia wear sarongs. These are lengths of cotton cloth which they wrap round their waists and wear with shirts or embroidered blouses.

Cold weather clothes

High in the Himalayan mountains, where the winters are bitterly cold, peoples' clothes are large and loose so they can wear lots of layers underneath. They are made of fur or thick felt and are often padded for extra warmth. The long, wide sleeves roll down to cover their hands, and ear-flaps protect their ears.

Hats and head-dresses

The light, straw, cone-shaped hats worn in South-East Asia, protect people from the sun and rain but are cool to wear.

A turban, like this man from Afghanistan is wearing, is a long piece of cloth wrapped round and round the head.

Arab men's head-dresses are plain white or have red or black patterns. The cloth is held on with a thick cord.

Village women in Bolivia wear felt bowler hats. These were first worn 50 years ago and were copied from Europeans.

3

People who live in deserts wear thin loose clothes to keep cool. This Tuareg tribesman from the Sahara covers his face and head too, for protection against the burning sun and blowing sand.

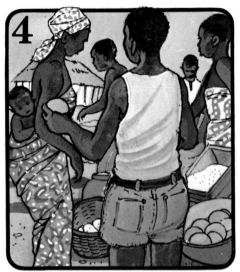

4

Women in many African countries wear brightly coloured cloths which they wrap round themselves. Some women wear western-style dresses made from this material.

5

Some of the tribal peoples who live in hot, rainy jungles wear only waistbands. They often rub coloured plant juices on to their skins to keep off insects.

1 Special clothes

In some Muslim countries women have to cover themselves from head to foot before going out. These Arab women from the Yemen wear long black robes and face masks.

2

Policemen, like this French *gendarme*, and soldiers, nurses and people in many other jobs, wear special uniforms so that they can be recognized.

3

The coloured head-dresses of these Kirghiz women from Russia have special meanings. Married women wear red and unmarried girls wear white.

4

The cross-stitch embroidery on this Arab woman's dress shows which town she comes from. Women from different towns have different embroidery.

Fashion

Elderly Japanese women still wear their traditional kimonos but younger girls wear modern fashion clothes. Fashion trends are much the same all over the world.

National costume

Sporran

Tartan kilt

This Scotsman is wearing his national costume. Most European countries have national costumes but they are worn only on special occasions or for tourists.

Ideas for dressing up

SARONG
1. SHEET OR MATERIAL ABOUT 2m LONG
SEW OR SAFETY PIN EDGES
2. FOLD ACROSS STOMACH AND TUCK IN AT WAIST
HOLD HERE
3. FOLD OTHER SIDE OVER
SAFETY PIN

SARI
1. LONG BIT OF MATERIAL e.g. OLD SHEET TORN IN HALF LENGTH WAYS WITH ENDS SEWN TOGETHER
TUCK EDGE INTO PANTS
2. BRING MATERIAL IN FRONT OF YOU AND FOLD TO MAKE 4 BIG PLEATS
TUCK INTO PANTS
3.
4. WIND MATERIAL BEHIND YOU, THEN UP OVER YOUR LEFT SHOULDER

TURBAN
1. LONG SCARF OR BIT OF OLD SHEET
2. WIND ENDS ROUND FRONT OF HEAD
3. TUCK ENDS IN AT BACK

Hair, jewellery and make-up

People arrange their hair, paint their faces and wear jewellery to make themselves more attractive to others. People from different parts of the world have very different styles of decorating themselves. What some people think beautiful, others, with different traditions, may find very ugly. Women usually dress themselves up more than men, but among some tribal peoples, the men often spend hours decorating themselves.

Jewellery

The silver bands and coins worn by this woman from Laos are her family's savings and show how rich they are.

This Amazon jungle woman wears seeds and monkey's teeth. People often make jewellery from things they find.

Indian women sometimes wear rings in their noses. This shows that they are married.

Sometimes jewellery shows a person's religion. This Christian girl wears a cross.

Masai women, who live in East Africa, wear many necklaces made from coloured glass beads. Some bind their arms and legs with metal rings, and it is shameful for a married woman to be seen without her earrings.

Hair and hairstyles

People of different races have different types of hair. You can see the three main types below.

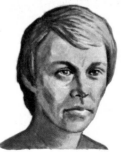

People of the Caucasoid race have straight or wavy hair. It may be blond, brown, reddish-brown or black.

Mongoloid people have thick, straight, black hair, and very little hair on their faces or bodies.

Negroes have dark, tightly curled hair. This probably developed as a protection against the hot sun.

In India, people think it is unfeminine for women to have short hair. They often wear it in long plaits. Young women are now breaking with this tradition and cutting their hair.

Make-up and body paint

Since prehistoric times people have painted and decorated their bodies. Over 5,000 years ago the Egyptians used eye make-up called kohl, made from a powdered rock. Kohl is still used in India and the Middle East.

Women all over the world use make-up. Modern make-up is made from chemical dyes and plant and animal oils.

This woman from the jungle in Peru paints her face with vegetable dyes. The patterns show which tribe she comes from.

At festival time, Huichol women from Mexico stick petals on their faces with lipstick so the gods know they want children.

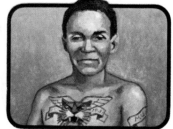

Sailors learned how to tattoo from Pacific islanders. The pattern is pricked into the skin and colour is rubbed in.

Since childhood, this woman from the Amazon jungle has worn little bits of wood stuck through her lips.

Hair plastered with beeswax and dusted with colour.

Mirror

Paint made from powdered rocks.

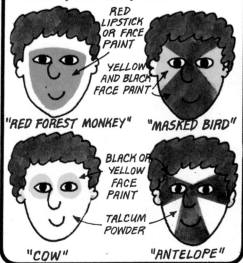

Men of the Nuba people, from Sudan, paint their bodies to make them look strong and healthy. They oil their skins and then colour them with powdered red or yellow rocks, black ashes or crushed white shells.

How to paint your face

Here are some Nuba face patterns you could try out. You can buy face paints at toy shops or theatre suppliers, or you could use old make-up. Use cold cream to remove your face paint.

RED LIPSTICK OR FACE PAINT

YELLOW AND BLACK FACE PAINT

"RED FOREST MONKEY"   "MASKED BIRD"

BLACK OR YELLOW FACE PAINT

TALCUM POWDER

"COW"   "ANTELOPE"

2

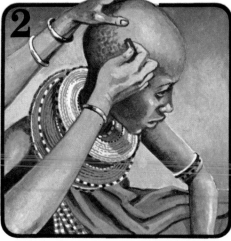

Masai women shave their heads to make themselves more beautiful and show off their colourful jewellery. They shave on special occasions with razor blades and a mixture of milk and water.

3

It is the Masai warriors who wear their hair long. They spend several days dressing each other's hair, coating it with a mixture of red soil called ochre and animal fat. They rub the strands together to make little twisted ropes of hair and gather them together with clips of wood. Masai men often put sweet-smelling leaves under their arms to make them smell nice. They, too, wear lots of jewellery.

Crafts

In many parts of the world people still make the things they need by hand. Some countries are famous for the work done by their craftsmen. Beautiful carpets are made in Iran, fine lace is made in Spain, Morocco is famous for its leather crafts and Indonesia for its silver work. Most craftsmen work with traditional tools and to patterns and designs that have been followed for hundreds of years. Nowadays they sell most of their work to tradesmen.

Weaving

Most cloth is now made in factories by machines, but some craftsmen still use hand looms to weave sheep's wool, goats' hair, cotton and silk into cloth.

1 Baskets

This English man is making a basket with willow sticks. Good baskets cannot be made by machines, so they are still made by hand all over the world.

Mexican women weave brightly coloured cotton cloth for clothes. Weaving is done on looms which hold the long "warp" threads tight while the coloured threads are woven in and out with wooden shuttles. This back-strap loom is easy to pack up and carry around.

Spinning

Cotton and wool must be spun into yarn before they can be woven. This Greek woman is spinning wool on a spindle.

2

Sticks, leaves, grasses and straw can all be woven to make baskets. This Kraho Indian woman from Brazil weaves baskets of palm leaves for carrying fruit.

Carpet making

In Turkey, carpets are made by knotting short pieces of wool on to the upright threads of wall looms. They are made by women and girls working at home. Carpets of different designs and colours are made in **different** regions.

Dyeing

The yarn is dyed with natural plant colours or chemical dyes. In Morocco, men dye wool in big pits or vats.

Pottery

Pottery is made from clay which is baked until it becomes hard. In many countries, local village potters make clay pots for the villagers to carry water or store food in.

Smooth, even pots are made by shaping the clay while it spins round on a wheel. This Turkish man works as a potter and sells his pots to shops in the towns.

In this pueblo village in the state of New Mexico, U.S.A., an Indian woman is shaping a pot from coils of clay. She smooths the coils together with her fingers. When the pot has been baked, she will paint on it special patterns which have been used in this region for hundreds of years. Villagers and tourists buy the pots.

Egyptian women buy huge pots from village potters to carry water from the well. Many of them do not have running water in their homes.

Batik

In Indonesia, patterns are made on cloth by a special method called *batik*. This woman is painting the pattern with melted wax from a wooden pen. When the cloth is dyed, the colour does not sink into the waxed areas. Later she paints more wax patterns and re-dyes the cloth to make beautiful and intricate patterns.

How to paint wax pictures

You can use the batik method to paint unusual pictures.

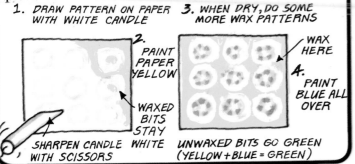

1. DRAW PATTERN ON PAPER WITH WHITE CANDLE

2. PAINT PAPER YELLOW

WAXED BITS STAY WHITE

SHARPEN CANDLE WITH SCISSORS

3. WHEN DRY, DO SOME MORE WAX PATTERNS

WAX HERE

4. PAINT BLUE ALL OVER

UNWAXED BITS GO GREEN (YELLOW + BLUE = GREEN)

Carving

Dutch craftsmen still carve wooden clogs by hand. They sell them to tourists as few people in Holland now wear clogs.

The wood carvings from West Africa are famous. This bird was carved by one of the Ashanti people, who live in Ghana.

Bark painting

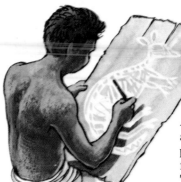

Australian Aboriginals are well-known for the paintings they do on bark from eucalyptus trees. This is a painting of a kangaroo.

Beliefs

People round the world have different beliefs and belong to different religions. On pages 84–87, you can find out about the main world religions followed by people from many different countries.*

Tribal peoples have their own religions and beliefs. As they are giving up their traditional ways of life, however, they are also changing their beliefs. Many tribal peoples now belong to one of the world religions, such as Christianity or Islam.

These flute players in the Amazon jungle pray to their gods with music. They are asking them to end the rainy season so they can start fishing again.

This Aboriginal man from Australia is doing a wind dance. The rustle of the leaves tied to his legs makes a sound like the wind which he hopes will bring fish to the shore.

Frightening off spirits

The Ho people in eastern India believe in spirits which live in plants. This priest is thanking the spirit of the harvest for protecting the crop, by offering it a cock.

Villagers in Nigeria leave food for the spirits of their ancestors at this shrine. They believe the spirits will bring bad luck if they are not looked after.

Some Chinese, especially in Hong Kong, believe that their ancestral spirits protect them. In return they offer food and burn incense at their graves.

Witchcraft

In this street market in South Africa you can buy medicines to keep away witches. Many tribal peoples in Africa believe that illness and misfortune can be caused by witches' spells.

This man from the Ivory Coast is a witch-finder. He looks into a bowl of water and sees the faces of witches who have put spells on people.

The magic things in this Angolan man's bowl help him to find witches. He shakes them and reads answers in the way they fall.

Some witch-finders use rubbing boards like this. They ask questions and slide the knob along the board. When it sticks, they know the answers.

*The chart on pages 92-95 shows the religions practised in each country.

Mask to frighten spirits.

Mask to hide person

Mask that looks like a bird.

For special ceremonies and dances, tribal peoples often wear masks. Sometimes these are to hide them from evil spirits, or frighten off dangerous ghosts. Other masks are worn so that people can talk to spirits without being recognized.

Ideas for making masks

Here are some ideas for making masks.

CARDBOARD MASK

1. CUT A PIECE OF CARD TO COVER YOUR FACE

EYE HOLES

STRING HOLES

MOUTH HOLE

2. PAINT AND DECORATE MASK

DRINKING STRAW MASK

STRING HOLES

BEND 10cm FROM END

EYE HOLES

BEND

1. CUT A STRIP OF CARD 50cm LONG, 10cm WIDE

PAPER TONGUE GLUED ON TO MASK

FEATHERS OR LEAVES

LONG STRAWS

STRING

CUT STRAWS TO FIT

2. STICK STRAWS ON WITH STICKY TAPE

Useful things for decorating masks: string, wool, raffia, paints, bottle tops, silver paper, feathers.

By the light of a full moon, these Karaja Indians from Brazil dance through their village dressed in coconut fibre and grasses. They stamp their feet and shake rattles to frighten away evil spirits.

The evil eye

Some people believe that sickness and bad luck can be caused by people looking at them with the "evil eye". To protect themselves they wear charms. People round the world have different superstitions. In Britain, horseshoes are believed to bring good luck.

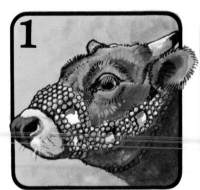

1

Blue beads, like those on the harness of this Greek bull, are supposed to ward off the evil eye. Silver charms shaped like hands are also supposed to give protection.

2

Fishermen in Portugal paint eyes on their boats. They are said to help them catch a lot of fish because the eyes can "see" where the fish are.

3

This Nuba girl from the Sudan, in Africa, wears special herbs in pouches round her neck. These keep away evil spirits and help to bring her good luck.

World religions

Judaism

Judaism is the religion of the Jewish people. There are about 12 million Jews. Over three million of them live in Israel, where Judaism began over 3,000 years ago.

Jews believe that there is one God and that they have a special duty to worship him. They believe that they are descended from a tribe of people called the Hebrews, and that God chose two of the Hebrew people, Abraham and Moses, to be his messengers.

Jews believe that God gave Moses the Ten Commandments, written on stone tablets. The Commandments are rules saying how people should live together and worship God.

This Rabbi, or Jewish teacher, is reading from the Jews' most holy book, called the Torah. The Torah is written by hand in the Hebrew language and Jews believe it contains God's words to Moses.

The Sabbath is a holy day for Jews. It begins on Friday at sunset, when Jewish families eat a special Sabbath meal and light the Sabbath candles. It ends when it gets dark on Saturday.

On the Sabbath Jews worship God in the synagogue. When boys are 13 and girls are 12 they should begin to live by the Jewish traditions. This is called the age of Bar-mitzvah.

This is the Western Wall in Jerusalem where Jews go to pray. It is the remains of an ancient temple which was destroyed over 2,000 years ago and is a very holy place for Jews.

Christianity

Christians believe that a man called Jesus Christ, born nearly 2,000 years ago, was the son of God.

When Jesus was born, some Jews believed he was the "Messiah", sent from God to bring peace on Earth. They became the first Christians. Followers of Jesus spread his teachings across the world and today, nearly a quarter of all the people in the world is Christian.

The life of Jesus is described in the New Testament, part of a book called the Bible which is holy to Christians. Jesus spent his life teaching about God and healing people. He chose 12 followers, or disciples, to be with him and carry on his work. Christians also believe, like Jews, that Abraham and Moses were messengers of God.

Islam

People who follow the religion of Islam are called Muslims. They believe there is one God whom they call Allah, and that the Prophet Muhammad, who was born 1,400 years ago in Mecca, Arabia, was the messenger of God. Muslims believe that Abraham, Moses and Jesus were also God's messengers. The followers of Muhammad spread the ideas of Islam through the Middle East. Today it is the main religion of all the Arab countries, and also of Pakistan and parts of Africa and South-East Asia.

Minaret—the tall tower of a mosque.

Religious symbols

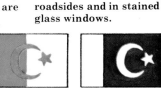

The Star of David, king of the Jews in Bible times, and the Menorah, a special candlestick, are Jewish symbols.

The cross is a Christian symbol. It can be seen in churches and shrines, by roadsides and in stained glass windows.

Turkey   Algeria   Pakistan

The crescent shape of a new moon is the symbol of Islam. Flags of many

Muslim countries have crescents and stars on them.

The Muslim holy book is called the Koran. Muslims believe the Koran is an account of God's words to Muhammad and it is always written in Arabic. This is a page from a very old Koran.

From the tall tower of a mosque, a man calls Muslims to prayer. They are supposed to pray five times a day. Before they go in to a mosque they should take off their shoes and wash.

If they are not near a mosque, Muslims can spread out prayer mats and say their prayers. They turn to face in the direction of the city of Mecca and recite from the Koran.

Building called the Kaaba.

Mecca is a holy place for Muslims. Once in their lives, if they can, they are supposed to make a pilgrimage to the city. There, they pray at the holy building called the Kaaba.

2

Jesus died by being crucified, which means he was nailed to a cross. In his lifetime he was loved and followed by many people, but some of the Jews feared his power.

Christians believe that Jesus rose from the dead and now lives with God in heaven. They believe that if they lead good lives, they too will go to heaven when they die.

3

On Sundays, Christians go to church to worship God. This picture shows the church of the Holy Sepulchre in Jerusalem which traditionally marks the place where Jesus was buried.

4

When people become Christians they promise to try and follow Jesus and are baptized. Most Christians are baptized when they are babies and their godparents make the promise for them.

Hinduism

Hinduism began about 4,000 years ago and is the oldest world religion. There are about 500 million Hindus, most of whom live in India.

Hindus believe in reincarnation, that is, they believe that when people die, they are born again into other bodies until they are good enough to be united with God. If people lead bad lives, they believe they may be reborn as animals.

Buddhism

Buddhism was started in India about 2,500 years ago by a man called Gautama who is known as the Buddha. He taught that suffering is caused by people's selfish behaviour and that if they try to lead good lives they will be happy and have peace of mind. Buddhists believe that they are born again and again into this world, until they reach Nirvana, a state of everlasting peace.

1

This is a statue of a Hindu god called Shiva, Lord of Dance. Hindus worship many gods and goddesses but they believe that each one represents a form of the highest God.

2

Hindus often have shrines in their homes, where they worship their gods. They pray and light candles at the shrines, make offerings of food and read stories about the gods from their holy books.

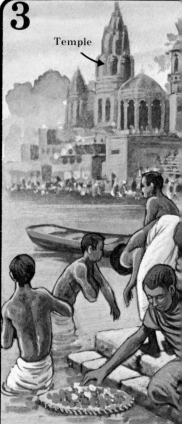

3

Temple

The River Ganges is a very sacred place for Hindus and they make pilgrimages to it. They wash away their sins in the water and float trays of flowers and incense on the river as offerings to the gods.

This is a golden statue of Buddha in front of which Buddhists meditate about his teachings. He wanted to be thought of as a guide and not as an idol to be worshipped.

To help them lead better lives and move nearer to Nirvana, Buddhists visit shrines where they make offerings of food and flowers and meditate on Buddha's teachings.

Begging bowl

Many Buddhist men live in monasteries for a few weeks and some spend their lives as monks. They shave their heads, wear yellow robes and carry begging bowls for food. They lead very simple lives and spend much time meditating. They also teach children about Buddhism and take care of funerals and other ceremonies. Buddhists believe that if they try and follow the example of the monks, it will help them reach Nirvana.

This wheel carved in stone is a Buddhist symbol. The eight spokes stand for the main points of Buddha's teachings.

4

When Hindus die their bodies are burned and the ashes are sprinkled in rivers. Their families pray that their souls will find their way to God and not be reborn again into this world.

5

Hindus have great respect for animals because they believe that everything has a soul. Cows are specially sacred and are allowed to wander freely in the streets.

The caste system

Every Hindu is born into a group called a caste. Some of the castes are thought to be higher and purer than others and priests come from the highest caste.

One of the most important Hindu duties is to obey caste rules. Different castes are supposed to do different work and they are not supposed to marry people from other castes.

Some people in India think the caste system is unfair and are trying to change it.

This man is a shoemaker and he is a member of one of the lowest castes, called the Harijans. Hindus believe that if they obey caste rules they may be reborn into higher castes.

Sikhism

This religion was begun by Guru Nanak, a spiritual leader who lived in India about 500 years ago. He taught that the caste system was wrong and that people should worship only one god. Today there are about 12 million Sikhs.

Sikhs worship God in their temples and read from the Granth, their holy book which contains the teachings of their leaders or "Gurus".

Sikh men and women are not supposed to cut their hair. The men wear turbans to keep it in place and silver bangles on their wrists.

Map of world religions

North America

Europe

Asia

Africa

South East Asia

South America

Australasia

Christianity
Judaism
Islam
Buddhism
Hinduism
Tribal religions
Chinese religions
Shinto
Christianity and tribal religions

Shinto

Shinto is an ancient religion which is practised in Japan. People worship spirits at shrines where they hang prayer notes and offer food and money.

Celebrations and festivals

All round the world, festivals are times when people dress up in their best clothes, eat special food and give presents.

In most countries, the main festivals celebrate special events in people's religions, such as the birth of a prophet. Other celebrations mark the coming of the new year, or special days such as birthdays.

Christmas

Every year on 25 December, Christians celebrate Christmas to remember the birth of Jesus Christ. Christians in different countries have their own special customs which take place during the Christmas season. Many have stories about St Nicholas, known as Santa Claus, who brings presents.

1 Holland

On 6 December, St Nicholas' Day, Santa Claus fills children's shoes with presents and takes the straw and carrots they leave for his horse.

2 Italy

Lady Befana brings gifts on 6 January. Legend says she was too busy to visit Jesus when he was born, so now she looks for him at every house.

3 Austria

People dress up in masks and straw to tease children. They pretend to be the companions of St Nicholas who used to punish naughty children.

4 Sweden

Early in the morning on St Lucia's day, 13 December, young girls wearing crowns of candles offer people special wheat cakes.

5 Mexico

Christmas decorations called pinatas are full of sweets and nuts. Children are blindfolded and have to try and break the pinatas with sticks.

Buddha's birthday

This Burmese girl is lighting candles to honour Buddha's birthday. Buddhists also celebrate the day a man becomes a monk.

New Year

New Year is celebrated on different days around the world because people use different systems to work out their calendars. In some countries the New Year begins on a different day each year.

Many New Year customs probably began as ways of chasing away the evil spirits of the old year and welcoming good fortune.

In parts of India, the Hindu New Year is marked by the Diwali festival. Patterns of rice flour on doorsteps welcome the goddess of wealth.

Chinese people all over the world celebrate their New Year with dragon dances and firecrackers to frighten away evil spirits.

Hindu festivals

There are many festivals in India as Hindus have lots of gods to honour. This is the "Car" festival for the god Juggernaut*, Lord of the Universe. Huge carts with statues of the god, attended by priests, are pulled through the streets.

Weddings

At Greek weddings, after the church ceremony, it is the custom for guests to pin paper money on the bride and bridegroom.

Arab Muslim marriages usually take place at home. A marriage contract is signed and then there is a party for relatives and friends.

In Hindu marriage ceremonies, the couple are joined with a white cloth. Parents usually choose whom their children should marry.

Jewish festivals

Jews celebrate many events believed to have happened in their history. The Passover festival reminds them of when Moses rescued their ancestors, the Israelites, from slavery over 3,000 years ago. The Israelites had to escape quickly and did not have time to let their bread rise. To remind them of this, Jews eat flat, unleavened bread, during Passover week.

For the Sukkot festival, people build little huts in their gardens. This reminds them of how their ancestors lived in the wilderness.

Muslim feast

During the month of Ramadan, Muslims are supposed to fast. They may not eat or drink during daylight hours. At the end of the month they feast and give presents.

May Day

On 1 May, May Day, parades of soldiers and people with red flags march through Red Square, in Moscow, U.S.S.R. They are celebrating the achievements of the working people.

How to make a pinata

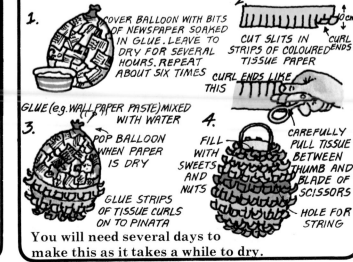

1. COVER BALLOON WITH BITS OF NEWSPAPER SOAKED IN GLUE. LEAVE TO DRY FOR SEVERAL HOURS. REPEAT ABOUT SIX TIMES

2. CUT SLITS IN STRIPS OF COLOURED TISSUE PAPER. CURL ENDS. CURL ENDS LIKE THIS. 10 cm

GLUE (e.g. WALLPAPER PASTE) MIXED WITH WATER

3. POP BALLOON WHEN PAPER IS DRY. GLUE STRIPS OF TISSUE CURLS ON TO PINATA

4. FILL WITH SWEETS AND NUTS. CAREFULLY PULL TISSUE BETWEEN THUMB AND BLADE OF SCISSORS. HOLE FOR STRING

You will need several days to make this as it takes a while to dry.

For Shinto weddings in Japan, the bride often wears a kimono and changes into modern clothes for the reception.

This is the origin of our word juggernaut, meaning large truck.

89

Music and dancing

In the past, people in Europe and America danced their traditional folk dances at fairs, festivals, weddings and celebrations. Folk dances are very old and the steps have been passed down from parents to children for hundreds of years. Nowadays they are mostly performed by dance groups in national costumes.

In other parts of the world, people have traditional dances which they perform at festivals or use to tell stories of their gods and heroes.

Balinese dancers

The flamenco dances of southern Spain are usually danced by gypsies to the music of guitars. They wear frilly skirts and make clicking sounds with castanets.

In Russian Cossack dancing, the men do somersaults and high kicks to show their skill. These dances were first done by Cossack soldiers several hundred years ago.

In India, Hindus worship their gods with dances. They use movements of their hands and eyes to tell stories about the gods.

On the island of Bali, in Indonesia, dancers act out stories about their Hindu gods with intricate movements of their eyes and bodies. Before the dances, which are often performed in temples, offerings of fruit and flowers are made to the gods. The dancers wear richly coloured silk costumes and head-dresses.

Balinese children begin to learn to dance when they are about six years old. It takes years of training to master the movements.

The dancers need perfect muscle control to perform the delicate hand and arm movements, all of which have special meanings.

This dancer is dressed up as the wicked witch, Rangda. Many of the dances are stories about the triumph of good over evil.

Musical instruments

Each region of the world has its own folk music which is played on traditional musical instruments to accompany folk dances.

The Spanish guitar probably developed from instruments like the Arabic "ud", shown on the right.

The Arabic ud is a kind of lute which is played by plucking the strings. It is used in classical and folk music.

The sitar is an Indian instrument which has six or seven strings. The person playing it sits on the floor and plucks the strings with their fingers.

Bagpipes are played to accompany Scottish sword dances. Air from the bag is forced through the pipes to make sounds.

In Indonesia, xylophones, gongs, bamboo pipes and drums are played in village orchestras.

Drums are often played in African music. Here they are being heated so that they make the right sounds.

4

Japanese Kabuki plays are a mixture of mime, music and dance. People offstage chant stories about ancient heroes and the actors wear traditional costume.

5

These Zulu men in South Africa are doing a warrior dance. In the past these were performed before battles, but now Zulus do them for tourists.

6

The Maori people of New Zealand dress up in their traditional clothes and dance on special occasions. Many of the dances tell stories of the Maoris' past.

Peoples of the world chart

PEOPLE	WHERE THEY LIVE	LANGUAGE	RELIGION	CURRENCY
Afghans	Afghanistan	Dari Persian, Pushtu	Muslim	Afghani (100 puls)
Albanians	Albania	Albanian	Muslim, Christian	Lek (100 qintars)
Algerians	Algeria	Arabic, Berber, French	Muslim	Dinar (100 centimes)
Americans	United States of America	English	Christian, Jewish	U.S. dollar (100 cents)
Andorrans	Andorra	Catalan, French, Spanish	Christian	French franc and Spanish peseta
Angolans	Angola	Portuguese, Bantu languages	Christian, tribal religions	Angolan escudo (100 centavos)
Arabs	Egypt, Syria, Jordan, Kuwait, United Arab Emirates, Oman, Saudi Arabia, Lebanon, Israel, Qatar, Bahrain, Libya, Tunisia, Algeria, Morocco, North and South Yemen	Arabic	Muslim	Money of countries where they live
Argentinians	Argentina	Spanish	Christian	Argentinian peso
Australians	Australia	English	Christian	Australian dollar (100 cents)
Austrians	Austria	German	Christian	Schilling (100 groschen)
Bahamians	Bahamas	English	Christian	Bahamian dollar
Bahrainis	Bahrain	Arabic	Muslim, Christian	Bahraini dinar
Bangladeshis	Bangladesh	Bengali	Muslim, Hindu, Christian, Buddhist	Taka (100 paisa)
Belgians	Belgium	French, Flemish, German	Christian	Belgian franc (100 centimes)
Belize, citizens of	Belize	English, American Indian languages	Christian, tribal religions	Belize dollar (100 cents)
Beninese	Benin	French, African languages: Fon, Adja, Bariba, Yoruba	Tribal religions, Christian, Muslim	Franc of the African financial community
Bhutanese	Bhutan	Dzongkha (a Tibetan dialect)	Buddhist, Hindu	Ngultrum (100 chetrum)

PEOPLE	WHERE THEY LIVE	LANGUAGE	RELIGION	CURRENCY
Bolivians	Bolivia	Spanish American Indian languages: Aymara, Quechua	Christian, tribal religions	Bolivian peso (100 centavos)
Botswanans	Botswana	Se-Tswana, English	Christian, tribal religions	South African rand
Brazilians	Brazil	Portuguese, American Indian languages	Christian, tribal religions	Cruzeiro (100 centavos)
British	United Kingdom	English, Welsh, Gaelic	Christian	Pound sterling (100 pence)
Bruneians	Brunei	Malay, Chinese, English	Muslim, Buddhist, Chinese religions	Bruneian dollar (100 cents)
Bulgarians	Bulgaria	Bulgarian, Turkish, Macedonian	Christian, Muslim	Lev (100 stotinki)
Burmese	Burma	Burmese, English	Buddhist, Muslim, Hindu, tribal religions	Kyat (100 pyas)
Burundi, citizens of	Burundi	French, African languages: Kiswahili, Kirundi	Christian and tribal religions	Burundi franc (100 centimes)
Cambodians: see Kampucheans				
Cameroonians	Cameroon	French, English, African languages	Tribal religions, Christian, Muslim	African financial community franc
Canadians	Canada	English, French	Christian	Canadian dollar (100 cents)
Cape Verdeans	Cape Verde Islands	Portuguese, Crioulo	Christian	Cape Verde escudo
Central African Empire, citizens of	Central African Empire	Sangho, French	Christian, tribal religions	African financial community franc
Chad, citizens of	Chad	French, Arabic, African languages	Muslim, Christian, tribal religions	African financial community franc
Chileans	Chile	Spanish	Christian	Chilean peso
Chinese	China, Taiwan, Hong Kong	Mandarin, other Chinese dialects, English	Buddhist, Chinese religions, Christian, Muslim	Yuan (100 fen), New Taiwan dollar, Hong Kong dollar
Colombians	Colombia	Spanish	Christian	Colombian peso
Comorians	Comoros	French, Comoran	Muslim, Christian	African financial community franc

PEOPLE	WHERE THEY LIVE	LANGUAGE	RELIGION	CURRENCY
Congolese	Congo	French, Bantu languages	Tribal religions, Christian	African financial community franc
Costa Ricans	Costa Rica	Spanish	Christian	Costa Rica colon
Cubans	Cuba	Spanish, English	Christian	Cuban peso
Cypriots	Cyprus	Greek, Turkish, English	Christian, Muslim	Cyprus pound
Czechoslovaks	Czechoslovakia	Czech, Slovak, Hungarian	Christian	Koruna (100 haleru)
Danes	Denmark	Danish	Christian	Danish Krone (100 øre)
Djiboutians	Djibouti	French, African languages	Muslim, Christian	Djibouti franc
Dominicans	Dominican Republic	Spanish	Christian	Dominican peso
Dutch	Netherlands	Dutch	Christian	Guilder (100 cents)
Egyptians	Egypt	Arabic	Muslim	Egyptian pound (100 piastres)
Ecuadoreans	Ecuador	Spanish	Christian	Sucre (100 centavos)
Equatorial Guineans,	Equatorial Guinea	Spanish, Fang, Bubi	Christian	Ekuele (100 centimos)
English	England	English	Christian	Pound sterling
Ethiopians	Ethiopia	Amharic, Galla, Somali	Muslim, Christian	Ethiopian dollar
Fijians	Fiji	English, Fijian, Hindi	Christian, Hindu	Fiji dollar (100 cents)
Filipinos	Philippines	Tagalog, English, local languages	Christian, Muslim, tribal religions	Filipino peso
Finns	Finland	Finnish, Swedish	Christian	Markka (100 pennia)
French	France	French	Christian	French franc (100 centimes)
Gabonese	Gabon	French and African languages: Fang, Eshira,	Christian, tribal religions	African financial community franc
Gambians	Gambia	English, African languages: Mandinka, Fula, Wollof	Muslim, Christian	Dalasi (100 butut)
Germans	East Germany, West Germany	German	Christian	East German mark (100 pfennige) Deutschmark (100 pfennige)
Ghanaians	Ghana	English, African languages	Christian, Muslim, tribal religions	New cedi (100 pesewas)
Gibraltar, people of	Gibraltar	English, Spanish	Christian	Gibraltar pound
Greeks	Greece	Greek	Christian	Drachma (100 leptae)

PEOPLE	WHERE THEY LIVE	LANGUAGE	RELIGION	CURRENCY
Grenadians	Grenada	English	Christian	East Caribbean dollar
Guatemalans	Guatemala	Spanish, American Indian languages	Christian	Quetzal (100 centavos)
Guineans	Guinea	French, African languages: Fulani, Susu, Malinke	Muslim, tribal religions	Syli (100 cauris)
Guinea-Bissauans	Guinea-Bissau	Portuguese, Creole, African languages: Balante, Fulani, Malinke	Tribal religions, Muslim	Guinean peso (100 centavos)
Guyanese	Guyana	English, Hindi, Urdu	Christian, Hindu	Guyanese dollar
Haitians	Haiti	Creole, French	Christian, Voodoo	Gourde (100 centimes)
Hondurans	Honduras	Spanish, American Indian languages	Christian	Lempira (100 centavos)
Hungarians	Hungary	Magyar	Christian, Jewish	Forint (100 filler)
Icelanders	Iceland	Icelandic	Christian	Icelandic Krona
Indians	India	Hindi and 15 other main languages	Hindu, Muslim, Christian, Sikh, Buddhist	Rupee (100 paisa)
Indonesians	Indonesia	Bahasa Indonesian, Javanese, Madurese, Sundanese	Muslim, Christian, Buddhist, Hindu	Rupiah (100 sen)
Iranians	Iran	Farsi	Muslim, Christian,	Iranian rial (100 dinars)
Iraqis	Iraq	Arabic, Kurdish,	Muslim, Christian	Iraqi dinar
Irish	Ireland	English, Gaelic	Christian	Irish pound (100 pence)
Israelis	Israel	Hebrew, Arabic, Yiddish	Jewish, Muslim	Israeli pound (100 agorot)
Italians	Italy	Italian	Christian	Italian lira
Ivory Coast, citizens of	Ivory Coast	African languages, French	Tribal religions, Muslim, Christian	African financial community franc
Jamaicans	Jamaica	English	Christian, Rastafarian	Jamaican dollar
Japanese	Japan	Japanese	Buddhist, Shinto	Yen (100 sen)
Jews	Israel and other countries	Hebrew, Yiddish or languages of countries where they live	Jewish	Money of countries where they live

PEOPLE	WHERE THEY LIVE	LANGUAGE	RELIGION	CURRENCY
Jordanians	Jordan	Arabic	Muslim, Christian	Jordanian dinar
Kampucheans	Kampuchea	Khmer, French	Buddhist	Riel (100 sen)
Kenyans	Kenya	English, African languages: Swahili, Kikuyu, Luo	Christian, tribal religions	Kenyan shilling (100 cents)
Koreans	North Korea, South Korea	Korean	Buddhist, Chinese religions, Christian	Won (100 jeon)
Kuwaitis	Kuwait	Arabic	Muslim, Christian	Kuwaiti dinar
Lao	Laos	Lao, French, English	Buddhist, tribal religions	Liberation kip (100 at)
Lebanese	Lebanon	Arabic, French,	Christian, Muslim	Lebanese pound (100 piastres)
Lesotho, citizens of	Lesotho	Sesotho, English	Christian	South African rand
Liberians	Liberia	English, African languages	Tribal religions	Liberian dollar (100 cents)
Libyans	Libya	Arabic	Muslim	Libyan dinar
Liechtenstein, citizens of	Liechtenstein	German	Christian	Swiss franc
Luxembourg, citizens of	Luxembourg	Letzeburgesch French, German	Christian	Luxembourg franc (100 centimes)
Malagasy	Malagasy Republic	Malagasy, French	Tribal religions, Christian, Muslim	Malagasy franc (100 centimes)
Malawians	Malawi	English, Nyanja	Tribal religions, Christian	Malawi kwacha (100 tambala)
Malaysians	Malaysia	Malay, English, Chinese, Indian languages	Muslim, Buddhist, Hindu, Christian	Ringgit (100 sen)
Maldivians	Maldives	Maldivian	Muslim	Maldivian rupee
Malians	Mali	Bambara, French	Muslim, tribal religions	Malian franc
Maltese	Malta	Maltese, English, Italian	Christian	Maltese pound (100 cents)
Mauritanians	Mauritania	French, Arabic	Muslim	Ouguiya (5 khoums)
Mauritians	Mauritius	English, Hindi, Creole, Urdu, French	Hindu, Christian, Muslim	Mauritian rupee (100 cents)
Mexicans	Mexico	Spanish	Christian	Mexican peso (100 centavos)
Monegasque	Monaco	French	Christian	French franc
Mongolians	Mongolia	Khalkha Mongolian, Russian	Buddhist	Tugrik (100 mongo)
Moroccans	Morocco	Arabic, Berber	Muslim, Christian	Dirham (100 centimes)

PEOPLE	WHERE THEY LIVE	LANGUAGE	RELIGION	CURRENCY
Mozambicans	Mozambique	Portuguese, African languages	Tribal religions, Christian, Muslim	Mozambican escudo (100 centavos)
Namibians	Namibia	Afrikaans, English, African languages	Christian, tribal religions	South African rand
Nauruans	Nauru	Nauruan, English	Christian	Australian dollar
Nepalese	Nepal	Nepali	Hindu, Buddhist, Muslim	Nepalese rupee (100 paisa)
New Zealanders	New Zealand	English, Maori	Christian	New Zealand dollar
Nicaraguans	Nicaragua	Spanish	Christian, tribal religions	Cordoba (100 centavos)
Niger, citizens of	Niger	French, African languages	Muslim, Christian, tribal religions	African financial community franc
Nigerians	Nigeria	English, African languages: Hausa, Ibo	Muslim, Christian, tribal religions	Naira (100 kobo)
Norwegians	Norway	Norwegian, Lapp	Christian	Norwegian krone (100 øre)
Omanis	Oman	Arabic	Muslim	Omani rial
Pakistanis	Pakistan	Punjabi, Urdu, Sindhi, Pushtu	Muslim, Hindu, Christian	Pakistani rupee (100 paisa)
Panamanians	Panama	Spanish	Christian	Balboa (100 centesimos)
Papua New Guineans	Papua New Guinea	English, Pidgin, Moru	Christian, tribal religions	Kina (100 toea)
Paraguayans	Paraguay	Spanish, American Indian languages	Christian, tribal religions	Guarani (100 centimos)
Peruvians	Peru	Spanish, American Indian languages: Quechua, Aymara	Christian, tribal religions	Peruvian sol (100 centavos)
Poles	Poland	Polish	Christian	Zloty (100 groszy)
Portuguese	Portugal	Portuguese	Christian	Portuguese escudo (100 centavos)
Qatar, citizens of	Qatar	Arabic	Muslim	Qatar riyal (100 dirhams)
Romanians	Romania	Romanian, Magyar, German	Christian	Leu (100 bani)
Russians: see Soviet Union				
Rwandese	Rwanda	French, African languages: Kinyarwanda, Kiswahili	Christian, Muslim, tribal religions	Rwandese franc (100 centimes)
Salvadoreans	El Salvador	Spanish	Christian	Colon (100 centavos)
San Marino, citizens of	San Marino	Italian	Christian	Italian lira

PEOPLE	WHERE THEY LIVE	LANGUAGE	RELIGION	CURRENCY
São Tomé and Príncipe, citizens of	São Tomé and Príncipe	Portuguese	Christian	Conto
Saudi Arabians	Saudi Arabia	Arabic	Muslim	Saudi riyal (100 halalah)
Scots	Scotland	English, Gaelic	Christian	Pound sterling
Senegalese	Senegal	French, African language: Wolof	Muslim, Christian, tribal religions	African financial community franc
Seychellois	Seychelles	Creole, English, French	Christian	Seychellois rupee
Sierra Leoneans	Sierra Leone	English, African languages: Krio, Mende, Temne	Tribal religions, Muslim, Christian	Leone (100 cents)
Singaporeans	Singapore	Malay, Mandarin Chinese, Tamil, English	Muslim, Buddhist, Hindu	Singaporean dollar (100 cents)
Solomon Islanders	Solomon Islands	Roviana, Marovo	Tribal religions, Christian	Solomon Island dollar
Somalis	Somalia	Somali, Arabic, English, Italian	Muslim, Christian	Somali shilling (100 centesimi)
South Africans	South Africa	Afrikaans, English, African languages: Xhosa, Zulu, Tswana, Sesotho, Sepedi	Christian, Muslim, Hindu, tribal religions	South African rand (100 cents)
Soviet Union, citizens of	Union of Soviet Socialist Republics	Russian, Ukranian, Byelorussian, Latvian, Lithuanian, Estonian, Georgian, Armenian, Uzbek and others	Christian, Muslim, Jewish	Rouble (100 kopeks)
Spaniards	Spain	Spanish	Christian	Peseta (100 centimos)
Sri Lankans	Sri Lanka	Sinhala, Tamil, English	Buddhist, Hindu, Christian, Muslim	Sri Lankan rupee (100 cents)
Sudanese	Sudan	Arabic, Nilotic	Muslim, tribal religions	Sudanese pound
Surinamese	Surinam	Dutch, Hindustani, Javanese, Creole	Christian, Hindu, Muslim	Surinamese guilder (100 cents)
Swazis	Swaziland	English, African language: Siswati	Christian, tribal religions	South African rand
Swedes	Sweden	Swedish, Finnish, Lapp	Christian	Swedish krona (100 ore)
Swiss	Switzerland	German, French, Italian, Romanche	Christian	Swiss franc (100 centimes)
Syrians	Syria	Arabic	Muslim, Christian	Syrian pound (100 piastres)
Tanzanians	Tanzania	English, African language: Swahili	Christian, Muslim, tribal religions	Tanzanian shilling (100 cents)
Thais	Thailand	Thai	Buddhist, Muslim	Baht (100 satangs)
Togolese	Togo	French, African language: Ewe	Tribal religions, Muslim, Christian	African financial community franc
Tongans	Tonga	Tongan, English	Christian	Pa'anga (100 seniti)
Trinidad and Tobago, citizens of	Trinidad and Tobago	English, Hindi, French, Spanish	Christian, Hindu, Muslim	Trinidad and Tobago dollar (100 cents)
Tunisians	Tunisia	Arabic, French	Muslim, Jewish, Christian	Tunisian dinar
Turks	Turkey	Turkish, Kurdish	Muslim	Turkish lira (100 kurus)
Ugandans	Uganda	English, African languages: Luganda, Ateso, Runyankore	Christian, Muslim, tribal religions	Ugandan shilling (100 cents)
United Arab Emirates, citizens of	United Arab Emirates	Arabic	Muslim	United Arab Emirates dirham (100 fils)
Upper Voltans	Upper Volta	French, African language: Mossi	Tribal religions, Muslim, Christian	African financial community franc
Uruguayans	Uruguay	Spanish, American Indian languages	Christian, tribal religions	New Uruguayan peso (100 centesimos)
Vatican City, citizens of	Vatican City	Italian, Latin	Christian	Italian lira
Venezuelans	Venezuela	Spanish	Christian	Bolivar (100 centimos)
Vietnamese	Vietnam	Vietnamese	Buddhist, Chinese religions, Christian	Dong (100 xu)
Welsh	Wales	Welsh, English	Christian	Pound sterling
Western Samoans	Western Samoa	Samoan, English	Christian	Tala (100 sene)
Yemenites	North Yemen South Yemen	Arabic Arabic	Muslim Muslim	Yemeni riyal Yemeni dinar
Yugoslavs	Yugoslavia	Serbo-Croat, Slovenian, Macedonian	Christian, Muslim	Yugoslav dinar (100 para)
Zairians	Zaire	French, African languages: Lingala, Kiswahili, Tshiluba, Kikongo	Tribal religions, Christian	Zaire (100 makuta)
Zambians	Zambia	English, African languages: Nyanja, Bemba, Tonga, Lozi, Lunda, Luvale	Christian, tribal religions	Zambian kwacha (100 ngwee)
Zimbabweans	Zimbabwe	English, African languages: Sindebele, Shona	Christian, tribal religions	Rhodesian dollar (100 cents)

Sports and games

Board games

Chess has been played for over a thousand years and probably began in India. It is a game for two people, played on a black and white chequered board.

Backgammon is played a lot in Greece and the Middle East. It is probably one of the world's oldest games and is played by two people with dice and 30 pieces.

Mah jong is an ancient Chinese game which has been played for over 2,000 years. Four people play, with little ''bricks'' traditionally made of bone, or ivory and bamboo.

Go is a very old Japanese game. It is played by two people with round black and white pieces on a low table marked out with squares.

Cards are used all over the world to play many different games. They were probably invented in China about 1,500 years ago.

Fighting

Judo developed from the ancient Japanese method of fighting called *ju-jutsu*. It first became an Olympic Games sport in 1964.

Karate is another Japanese method of fighting. To avoid injury when it is played as a sport, punches, blows and kicks are pulled back before touching the opponent.

Boxing matches were held in the ancient Greek Olympic Games. The rules of the modern game were drawn up in 1867 by the Marquis of Queensberry of England.

Thai boxing is popular in Thailand and Japan. Opponents are allowed to punch, kick, knee and elbow each other and also to use leg throws.

Fencing is a sport which developed from sword fighting. Opponents wear protective clothing and are not allowed to hit each other below the waist.

Football

Games in which stuffed leather balls were kicked around were played in China 2,000 years ago. **Soccer** is played by 2 teams of 11 players.

Rugby is played by 2 teams of 13 or 15 players. The ball is kicked or carried and points are scored by putting the ball over the goal line or kicking it over the crossbar.

In **American football,** players wear helmets and padding. Teams of 11 players tackle their opponents to stop them scoring by kicking goals or reaching the goal line.

Australian rules is played on an oval pitch by two teams of 18 players. Points are scored by kicking the ball between the opposite team's posts.

Gaelic football is played in Ireland by two teams of 15 players who try to score points by putting the ball in or over their opponent's goal. Players catch, fist and kick the ball.

Other ball games

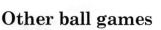

Lacrosse is played in Europe and N. America and developed from a game played by North American Indians.

Hockey is played with curved sticks by teams of 11 players. In Canada, teams of five play hockey on ice.

Modern **cricket** developed in England and is played by two teams of 11 players which take turns to bat and score points with runs.

Golf, as it is played today, developed in Scotland. A small hard ball is hit with a stick called a club into small holes on the golf course. Usually played by two people.

Tennis developed from a French game called handball. It is played by two or four players who hit a ball backwards and forwards over a net with their rackets.

Basketball is an American game in which two teams of five players try to throw the ball into the opposite team's ''basket''. The ball may be bounced or thrown.

American **baseball** developed from the English game of rounders. Teams of 9 players hit the ball with a wooden bat and score points by running round the ''bases''.

Pelota is a Spanish game played in a three-walled court. Players hit the ball with a special wicker basket and score points if their opponent misses the ball.

The French game of **boules** is played by throwing metal balls so that they land near a small marker ball. Players score points for balls nearest to the marker.

Billiards, a game played on a table with three balls which are hit with a stick, developed in England. Variations of the game are snooker and pool.

Part Four
Houses Around the World

Houses through the ages

1 About 350,000 years ago

In prehistoric times people hunted wild animals for food. They often followed the animals from place to place and camped a few days in huts built from branches and grass.

2 About 7,000 years ago

Later, when people learned how to plant crops and tame animals, they no longer needed to hunt. They settled down and built more solid houses. Some used mud baked hard by the sun.

3 About 3,500 years ago

Gradually the villages grew and became towns. In this crowded city in ancient Egypt, people lived in houses four or five storeys tall, as they were short of building space. They paid specially trained

5 About 900 years ago

In the early Middle Ages, country people lived in cottages made of "wattle and daub". They made a wooden frame and then filled it in with woven sticks (the wattle) and mud paste (the daub).

6 About 900 years ago

The Normans, who came from France, used stone for building. Their houses had outside staircases. You can spot a Norman building by its rounded door and window arches.

7 About 600 years ago

Town houses in the Middle Ages were built very close together. The upstairs rooms overhung the street and almost touched. There were no drains and people threw their rubbish into the street.

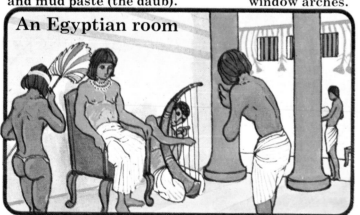

An Egyptian room

Egyptian houses, especially wealthy people's, were large and spacious. Small, high windows let in light and cool breezes, but kept out the glare of the hot summer sun. Guests were entertained in this hall.

Inside a peasant's cottage

Forests covered much of Europe in the Middle Ages, so wood was used for houses, furniture and even plates and bowls.

Cottage floors were bare earth, trodden down hard, and animals shared the living room. The fire made the room smoky.

builders to construct their houses, using sun-dried bricks made of mud and chopped straw. The bricks were smoothed over with a thin mixture of mud and water and sometimes painted.

8 About 150 years ago

When machines and factories were invented, thousands of workers moved to the cities. Rows of brick houses, with small back yards and outside toilets, were built for them to live in.

About 2,000 years ago

4

Walls cut away so you can see inside

Stairs to bedroom

Main living room

Bedroom

Kitchen

Dining room diners lay on couches

Fireplace for under-floor heating

Slaves gardening

Wealthy Romans lived in large villas like this. Whole streets of Roman houses have been found at Pompeii in Italy. They were preserved in ash from the volcano Vesuvius. These houses show that the Romans made bricks and roof tiles from clay baked in a fire, and that they had under-floor, hot-air central heating, baths and inside toilets.

A Norman hall

Wooden shutter

Norman houses were cold and draughty because they had no glass in the windows. The only heat came from a log fire in a huge stone fireplace in the wall. This is the hall where everyone ate and slept. The kitchen was in a separate building.

An old kitchen

Factory workers' houses a hundred years ago had no bathrooms. People washed in tin baths in the kitchen. They heated water on the cooking stove, which had a wood or coal fire burning inside it. Oil or gas lamps lit their rooms.

Mud huts and round houses

In hot, dry countries, mud is still used for building houses. It is mixed with straw to bind it together and either made into bricks or moulded into walls. The sun bakes the mud rock-hard. In many parts of the world it is a good, easy-to-find material for building with.

Many of the village houses in Africa are built of mud. They are cool inside because the thick mud walls keep out the sun. Mud houses are often round, because their walls are less likely to crack than if they had corners.

Plan of Nabdam house

Mud village

Mud huts in Botswana have wide thatched roofs to keep rain off the walls. Some people have built cement houses and bought modern furniture, such as beds, which do not fit in the round houses.

These round mud huts are the homes of a people called the Nabdam who live in northern Ghana. Each family owns a group of huts joined by walls, and when the sons marry, new rooms are added for their wives. The women usually decorate the houses, by making grooves in the mud and painting them with coloured vegetable juices.

Nabdam houses have very low doorways with no doors. Just inside the doorway is a low wall which keeps out the animals, wind and rain, but lets air in.

Bushmen

In the Kalahari Desert in southern Africa, there are Bushmen who still live by hunting. They camp at night in small, round huts built of sticks and grass.

1 Moving to the city

Making an animal from a vegetable

Many Africans are now moving to the cities, where they hope to find jobs and earn more money. Houses are too expensive for them to buy when they first arrive. In some cities, they can buy a plot of land with piped water and a toilet, and build a mud house. Later on, when they can afford it, they can have a modern cement house built.

Masai houses

Masai men playing a game with pebbles and a wooden tray.

Inside a Masai house

Screen

Cut-away wall

There are often no windows in Masai houses and the only light comes from the cooking fire. A woman builds her own house and lives there with her children. She sleeps behind the screen, on a bed of branches. Her husband may have several wives and not live with her all the time.

The Masai people live by herding cattle in East Africa. They build long, low houses of branches plastered with cow dung, which dries to form a hard, waterproof layer.

Several families and their cattle herds live together in a village protected by a fence of prickly thorn branches. Every day, the older boys take the cattle out to graze, and bring them back to the village before nightfall.

In this busy street in an African town, there are mud houses with thatched roofs, side-by-side with modern blocks of flats. The mud houses are probably the homes of newcomers to the city.

Some of the houses now have iron roofs instead of thatch, because they do not need repairing so often. Iron-roofed houses are hot inside though, because the metal heats up in the sun.

Vegetable animals
Here are some ideas for making animals from vegetables, as the boy in picture 1 is doing.

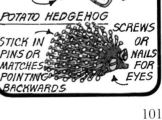

WASP CARROT
PAINT STRIPES
HOOPS OF WIRE COVERED WITH SELLOTAPE
USED MATCHSTICKS

POTATO HEDGEHOG
STICK IN PINS OR MATCHES POINTING BACKWARDS
SCREWS OR NAILS FOR EYES

Living in the jungle

Jungle, or rainforest, is hot and steamy and thick with plants and trees which grow very large because it rains heavily nearly every day. People who live there have to clear away the jungle growth before they can build houses or plant crops.

Much of the world's jungle has been cut down to make space for cities and farms. The largest jungle is around the Amazon river, in South America, where most of the people shown here live.

Giant round house

Deep in the Amazon jungle in Brazil and Venezuela, the Yanomamo Indians live under great circular roofs, like this. As many as 125 people live under each roof.

Inside a Yanomamo house

These boys are practising shooting arrows into a dummy made of palm leaves.

Bread is baked on a heated iron plate over a fire in the central area of the house.

This girl is making a waistband from the brightly coloured petals of jungle flowers.

With their faces smeared with war paint, these boys are pretending to raid an enemy camp as their fathers used to do.

Palm leaf houses

The Yawalapiti Indians of Brazil live in large palm-thatched houses in clearings in the jungle. About 30 people live together in one house and there are four or more houses in each village. The houses have no windows so they are dark and stuffy inside. The Yawalapiti live by hunting, fishing and growing a few crops.

102

The Mbuti people live in the jungle in Zaire, Africa. They are Pygmies, a race of people who are only about 130cm tall. They live mainly by hunting and gathering.

At night they sleep in round huts made of branches and sticks covered with large jungle leaves. The leaves keep out the rain, but easily catch fire when dry, so the Mbuti light fires outside their houses. On cold nights they sleep outside beside the fire.

The Yanomamo people sleep in hammocks and store their few possessions in the roof. Each Yanomamo family has its own area under the roof. The roof is made from the leaves of palm trees, laid in layers over a framework of poles. Cool breezes blow in through a narrow gap between the roof and the ground. About every two years, when the roof starts to leak or is full of insects, the Yanomamo burn it down and build a new one.

Jungle houses in Peru

These Amahuaca people of Peru are cutting back the jungle to make a clearing where they will put up a new house.

They lash sticks together to build a wooden frame which they thatch with palm leaves.

This Amahuaca woman is making a pot from coils of clay. Women plant and harvest the crops and also prepare the food.

This is a small jungle town on the Amazon river. The houses are built on stilts or rafts to protect them from floods.

Tents and caravans

Wooden pins

Cheese made from goats' milk drying in the sun.

Bedding

Pounding coffee beans to fine grains for making small cups of bitter black coffee.

Churning milk in a goatskin to turn it to butter.

Flour and water dough being made into flat loaves of bread.

Grinding wheat to make flour.

Some Bedouin keep a few hens for their eggs.

The Bedouin are Arabs who wander across the Arabian desert, herding camels, goats and sheep. They live in tents made of cloth woven from goat hair. Each tent has a dividing curtain.

On one side is the women's area where the family sleeps and the women cook. On the other side, the men receive their guests and hold meetings. When men from

outside the family visit the tent, all the women hide. They hang another curtain from the tent rope so the men cannot see into their part of the tent.

Gypsy caravans

This gypsy family are camping beside the road in their horse-drawn caravan. Gypsies are descended from travelling people who came from India. Now they live all over Europe and the Middle East.

In this caravan there is an old-fashioned wood-burning stove for cooking. Cupboards and walls have traditional decorations.

Most gypsies now live in modern caravans. They camp by the roads or on special gypsy campsites.

The side cloths are pinned to the roof and can be lifted to let in the breeze.

Coffee pot

Coffee cups

Inside the tent, the Bedouin sit on carpets. They have no furniture. When the guests arrive they bring out cushions for them to sit on.

How to make a tent

Here are some ideas for making tents indoors and outside.

WASHING LINE TENT

CLOTHES-HORSE TENT

BLANKET

PEGS

PEGS OR PINS

STONES

TWO BLANKETS

BACK OF SOFA TENT

TWO-CHAIR TENT

BOOKS FOR WEIGHT

CUSHION

BLANKET

TORCH FOR LIGHT

BOOKS

CUSHIONS TO SIT ON

NEVER light a fire inside your tent.

These are some useful things for making tents: broomsticks, blankets, safety pins, books, cushions, stones.

1 Living in yurts

The Turcoman live in the desert in Iran, travelling from place to place in search of water and pastures. They live in tents called yurts, which they carry with them on their camels.

The Turcoman women pitch the yurts. They put up a wooden frame first, then cover it with pieces of felt. In winter they use several layers of felt to keep out the cold.

There are three areas inside the yurt: one for sleeping, one for the women and one for the men. The bedding is stored in the sleeping area at the back of the tent.

Clothes and cooking pots are hung on the women's side. Weaving equipment, bags of wheat and flour, saddles and guns are kept on the men's side.

Turcoman women make the felt for covering the yurts, and for carpets and saddle bags too. The felt is made from sheep's wool. The young girls comb out the wool. Then the women wet it and roll

and press it between reed mats until the wool becomes tangled and matted to form felt. They make carpets and bags with coloured patterns, but wall felts are white until fire smoke blackens them.

Ranches and farmhouses

Thatched farmhouse

This painted English farmhouse has changed very little since it was built about 300 years ago. It was made of local stone and thatched with straw. The farmer and his family still live in it. The cowsheds, barns for hay, animal feed and farm machinery surround the yard. Many farms are in the middle of their fields, away from other houses.

A Danish farmhouse

Old farmhouses in Denmark, like this one, were once the home of the farmer, his family and his animals. Now sheds and stables have been built for pigs, cattle, hay and machinery, round a yard at the back of the house. The animals are kept indoors from October to May when it is too cold for grazing. This farmhouse also has rooms for farm workers and summer guests.

Spanish farming village

Farmhouses in Spain are often built close together on the steep hillsides. This leaves the flat land in the valley clear for farming. On the ground floor are stables and a grape press for making wine. The farmer and his family live on the next floor. The top floor is used for store rooms.

A farm in Argentina

In the countryside round the city of Cordoba, in Argentina, farmers have small houses built of mud bricks (sometimes called "adobe"). This farmhouse is surrounded by a fence to form a yard called a corral, where cattle, pigs and hens are kept at night. In the corral there is an oven, where the farmer's wife bakes her bread, and a well which provides drinking water. The farmer owns a small plot of land nearby where he grows vegetables and a few orange trees.

Farmers coming home from fields.

Grapevines

Drying sheep's wool

Drying vegetables

1 Life on a sheep station

Windmill

Sheep farms on the dry grasslands of Australia cover thousands of square kilometres. Farming families are often more than a day's drive from their nearest neighbours. Water has to be pumped up from underground streams by windmills. Supplies and letters come by plane.

2

Ranch-hands often ride motorbikes now, instead of horses, when they round up the sheep. They are helped by sheepdogs.

3

Children living on remote stations have lessons by two-way radio. They write their homework and post it to their teachers.

1 On a cattle ranch

In the Rocky Mountains, in Montana, U.S.A., cattle ranches are huge. In winter, hay is taken by horse-drawn sledges to feed the cattle. The cowboys live in wooden bunk houses near the ranch house. They now drive the cattle to market in large trucks, rather than herding them along the old cattle trails.

2

In spring the cowboys take the cattle up to the mountains looking for grass for grazing. They live in wooden cabins and cook over campfires.

Living on water

The Bajau people live on boats which they sail round the islands of South-East Asia. They are sometimes called sea gypsies.

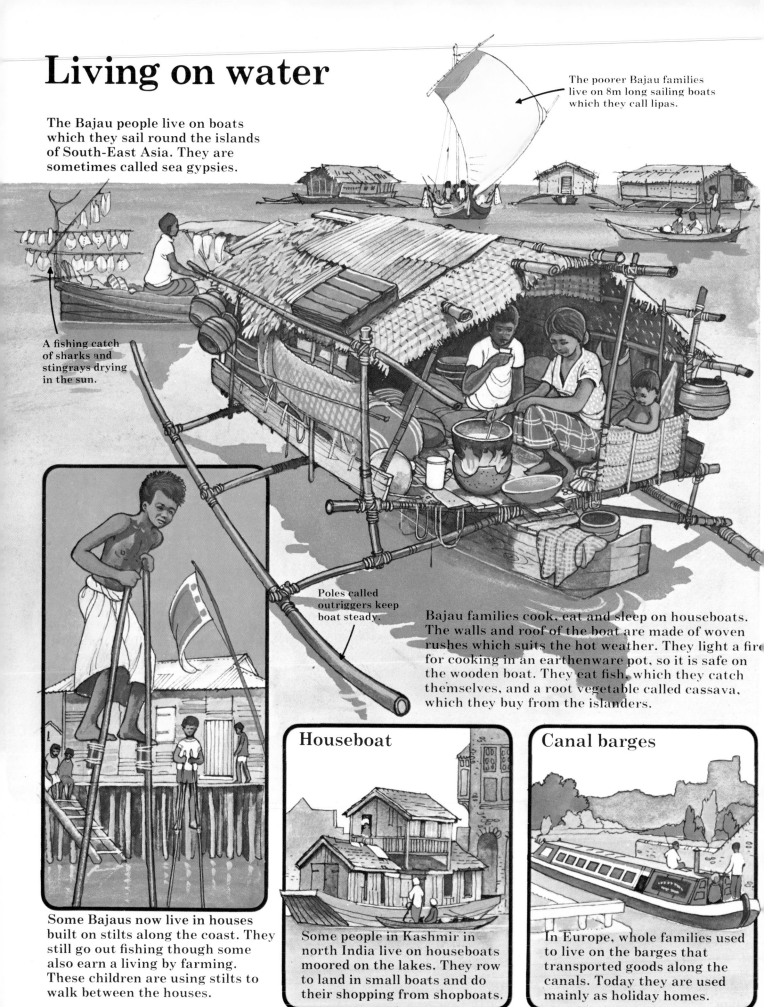

The poorer Bajau families live on 8m long sailing boats which they call lipas.

A fishing catch of sharks and stingrays drying in the sun.

Poles called outriggers keep boat steady.

Bajau families cook, eat and sleep on houseboats. The walls and roof of the boat are made of woven rushes which suits the hot weather. They light a fire for cooking in an earthenware pot, so it is safe on the wooden boat. They eat fish, which they catch themselves, and a root vegetable called cassava, which they buy from the islanders.

Some Bajaus now live in houses built on stilts along the coast. They still go out fishing though some also earn a living by farming. These children are using stilts to walk between the houses.

Houseboat

Some people in Kashmir in north India live on houseboats moored on the lakes. They row to land in small boats and do their shopping from shopboats.

Canal barges

In Europe, whole families used to live on the barges that transported goods along the canals. Today they are used mainly as holiday homes.

108

Houses in the marshes

On the vast marshlands between the Tigris and Euphrates rivers in southern Iraq, live people known as Marsh Arabs. They keep buffaloes, grow rice and catch fish in the lagoons.

Island of reeds and mud

Reed fence

Building a new house

Building a boat

Children playing with water buffaloes.

Drying buffalo dung which will be used for fuel.

Women cooking

The Marsh Arabs build their houses with reeds. There is little firm land in the marshes, so first they have to make an island, by fencing off part of the swamp and filling it in with rushes and mud.

Building a reed house

1

Bundles of giant reeds, cut from the marshes, are tied together and bent into a framework for the house. Ancient carvings show that this method of building was used here over 5,000 years ago.

2

Weaving wall mats

The walls and roofs of the Marsh Arabs' houses are made of mats woven from reeds. They sell spare mats in the local village markets. New wall mats have to be woven every few years as the reeds rot.

3

The houses are quite warm in winter as the matting keeps out the wind. Warmth from the fire dries out the reeds. In summer the walls are rolled up to let in the breeze.

109

Tree houses

In this look out, 12m up in the trees, men in India watched for enemies. Tree houses are not used as permanent homes, because it is very difficult to get water, food and firewood from the ground to the house. They are also easy for enemies to beseige or burn down.

Among some tribal peoples in New Guinea, young unmarried girls sometimes had to live in tree houses, and special ceremonies were held in them. Some even had fireplaces inside, made of clay or stone so they did not burn the house down.

Tree-stump house

The stump of this giant redwood tree has made a good solid platform for a house. It is used as a holiday house by its American owners.

Tree hide-out

This tree is big enough for four people to sit inside comfortably.

Baobab trees have extremely thick trunks. This one, which is in Africa, was hollowed out a long time ago as a hiding place during a war between two tribes. Since then, hunters have often sheltered in it and now it is a local landmark.

Building a tree house

If you want to build a treehouse, remember, it could damage the tree, so you should ask permission of the tree's owner first. If you live near an adventure playground, you could ask the playground leader if you could build a treehouse there. Never take candles or light a fire in a treehouse.

Living in caves

In 1971 a forest hunter called Dafal discovered some people called the Tasaday, living in caves in a remote valley in the Philippines. The entrances to their caves were high up in the rocks. To reach them they climbed trees or swung across on the long, rope-like stems of jungle plants.

When Dafal found them, the Tasaday were wearing clothes made from leaves, and using stone tools. They lived on wild plants and flowers, grubs, lizards, crabs and snakes.

1 Cave houses in Turkey

Pigeon houses

This strange landscape of cone-shaped rocks is in Turkey. The rock is soft and easy to carve, and for over 2,000 years local people have built their houses, churches and monasteries in the rocks. They hollowed out the cones and put in wooden windows and doors. When the rock is exposed to the air, it hardens.

2

Inside their cave homes, the people cover the earth floors with carpets and paint the rocky walls. They have carved rock staircases which lead to more rooms upstairs.

French caves

These old caves in France have been made into modern homes by building on new fronts with windows and doors and adding chimneys.

High in the mountains

There are people living in even the highest mountain ranges of the world. It is cold and desolate there and they need sturdy, thick-walled houses to protect them.

These are prayer flags, hung on the roof to bring good luck.

Firewood is stored here on the roof.

Poorer families use oiled paper instead of glass in the windows.

This girl is spinning a prayer wheel as she recites prayers of the Buddhist religion.

This is the only doorway everyone has to go through the yak stable to get into the house.

These are the Lobas people, who live among the snow-capped peaks of the Himalayas in Nepal. The highest mountain in the world, Mount Everest, is not far away. There are no trees to shelter them from the wind, because it is too cold for them to grow.

This family's house is built of stone and mud-brick. The ground floor is used as a stable and heat from the animals' bodies helps keep the house warm. The people live upstairs. They farm a few crops and keep sheep, goats, and mountain animals called yaks.

Yaks carry heavy loads and pull ploughs. Their hair is used for clothing and their dung for fuel. The females called dris, supply milk, butter and cheese.

1 Mexican mountain farm

The Huichols are American Indians who live in the mountains of western Mexico. It gets bitterly cold in winter, though trees and cacti still grow there. They live in isolated family groups on farms called "ranchos", several hours' walk from each other. Here, the Huichols are holding a ceremony to wish the men good luck when they travel into the mountains.

Good luck crosses

112

Inside the house, the family has a wood-burning stove for cooking food. There is also a bamboo churn for brewing tea, which they drink with butter and salt.

Some families now have more modern equipment, such as thermos flasks and pressure cookers. They buy these on rare trading expeditions to the towns.

This is a demon trap. The Lobas hang these over their doorways to keep away evil spirits. Round the ram's skull is a picture of each person living in the house.

In summer, the Lobas leave their isolated houses and meet other families for parties and picnics. They camp in tents like this one.

2

The ranchos are groups of huts made from stone and adobe (mud bricks). The thatched roofs overhang the walls to protect them from heavy rain.

This hut is used for cooking. These Huichol are making "tortillas", thin flat pancakes made with maize, which they eat instead of bread or rice.

Good luck crosses

To make good luck crosses like the Huichols, you will need some straws and wool.

1. TWO DRINKING STRAWS
TIE STRAWS TOGETHER WITH WOOL
TIE ON BALL OF WOOL

2. WIND WOOL ROUND LIKE THIS

3. REPEAT PROCESS HERE... ...AND HERE

Wooden houses and log cabins

1 Swiss chalets

In Switzerland, houses built of wood, like the farmhouse shown above, are called chalets. In the mountains and forested valleys, most of the houses are wooden.

In winter, the ground floor is used as a stable. This part of the house is built of stone so the damp does not rot it. The snow on the gently sloping roof helps to keep heat in.

Almost everything inside the chalet is made of wood, so there are strict laws about fire safety. The windows have double layers of glass to keep the house warm.

Old Japanese farmhouse

Inside the Japanese farmhouse, the family sleeps on a wooden platform covered with straw mats. In the past, there were no stables, and the animals slept in here too.

Trays of silkworms

This is an old-fashioned farmhouse in Japan. It is built of wood and thatched with reeds. There is no glass in the windows. Instead they are covered with screens made of straw and sliding wooden shutters which keep out the snow. The two small buildings in front of the house are where animals are kept. This is called a Minka farmhouse.

The attics are mainly used for growing silkworms. At both ends there are windows to let in the sunlight.

114

3

Haystacks

Winter houses in valley

Firewood

Cows wear bells so their owners can find them.

In summer, when the snow melts, the villagers move higher up the mountains to find good grass for their cows and to harvest hay ready for the winter.

While they are there they live in log cabins roofed with stones from the mountain quarries. These are much smaller and simpler than their winter homes in the valleys.

They cut the long grass, stack it and leave it to dry into hay. Before the winter snows come they take the hay and the animals back down the mountain.

Building wooden houses

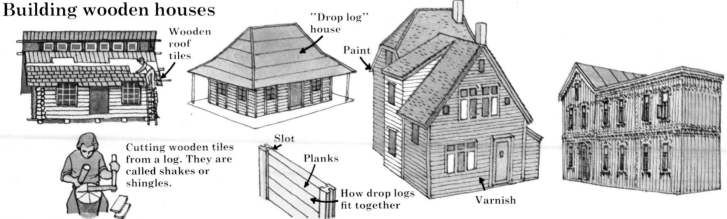

Wooden roof tiles

"Drop log" house

Paint

Cutting wooden tiles from a log. They are called shakes or shingles.

Slot

Planks

How drop logs fit together

Varnish

This cabin is made of logs which are fitted together at the corners in a criss-cross pattern. It is being roofed with wooden tiles.

In this house the planks of wood are fitted into slots in the upright posts. These are called "drop log" houses.

Wooden houses have to be treated against insects and painted or varnished regularly, to prevent the wood from rotting.

Some older wooden houses are decorated with carvings like this one in eastern USSR.

Living in icy places

The coldest places on Earth are the arctic lands near the North Pole, and Antarctica, the land at the South Pole. The winters are very long and the summers are warm, but short. For most of the year the land and sea are covered with thick snow and ice. In winter, it is daylight for only a few hours each day, but in summer the days are very long.

The Lapps

The Lapps live in the arctic lands of Norway, Finland, Sweden and Russia. Their clothes are embroidered with different patterns depending on the area they come from.

In the past they lived by hunting and herding reindeer. Nowadays most Lapps live and work in small towns.

A few Lapp families still keep herds of reindeer. In spring, they leave their homes and travel with the animals to the coast to escape the heat and insects of summer. On the way, they live in tents which they carry with them on their sledges. Some Lapp herders now use snow-mobiles instead of sledges.

Inside a Lapp tent

Lapp herdsman lining his fur boots with dried grass to keep his feet warm.

Lapp tents are made from sticks, covered with reindeer skins. They lay branches on the frozen ground inside the tent and cover them with fur rugs to keep out the cold.

1 Living in frozen Antarctica

Ice breaker supply ship

The only people who live in Antarctica are scientists and explorers. All their food and supplies have to be taken to them by ship or plane.

During the long winter no ships or planes can reach Antarctica. It is so cold and windy that the scientists cannot go outside.

2

This "Sno-cat" is going to a research station which is in a tunnel 10m down in the ice.

3

In spring, when the first ship breaks through the ice, it brings letters and parcels from home.

1 Eskimo houses

Teams of husky dogs pull sledges

Seal skin being cleaned

Eskimos used to live by hunting seals and whales. Now most of them work in towns and go hunting in their spare time for seal skins to sell. They live in Greenland, and in northern Canada, Alaska and Russia.

In these freezing lands, the Eskimos build their houses of wood and line them with fibreglass so that they stay warm inside. They build on rocks or oil drums sunk in the ice so the houses stay firm if the surface ice melts.

They carry supplies of dried food which they cook over the fire in the tent. At night they wrap themselves in reindeer skins and lie down near the fire. Some Lapps now have modern canvas tents.

2

In the past, when Eskimos went hunting, they lived in igloos which they built with blocks of snow. Nowadays the hunters take tents with them or stay in huts.

3

It was quite warm inside the igloos. The icy walls were covered with fur rugs. Lamps burning whale oil gave off heat and light.

Eskimo hunter

This Eskimo hunter is hiding behind a white screen so the animals cannot see him against the snow. The hunters use rifles now instead of spears.

An Eskimo game

This game was good practice for spear-throwing. Eskimo children made little wooden spears and tried to thrust them through a ring made of bone.

1. GLASS
CARD
DRAW ROUND GLASS AND CUT CIRCLE OUT OF CARD

2. COIN
CARD CIRCLE
DRAW ROUND COIN AND CUT OUT CENTRE OF CARD CIRCLE

3. ROLL A SHEET OF NEWSPAPER TO MAKE A "SPEAR"

4. PAPER SPEARS

Living together

Palm thatch roof

Bedding mats

Ladder carved from a log

A kibbutz

Children's house

Lessons outdoors

1 Chinese commune

These caves used to be houses, but are now pigsties.

A kibbutz is a village in Israel where everyone has a share in the land and property of the village. They work and eat together and meet to discuss kibbutz affairs. Sometimes children live in special houses, away from their parents.

Taichai village is part of a Chinese commune, where everyone works together on the land. They share the produce among themselves and with the other villages in the commune. Flat "terraces" have been cut into the hillsides to make farmland.

118

Underground houses

Washing clothes

Devil scares

Pounding rice

In the dense jungle on the island of Borneo, people called the Dayaks live in longhouses like this one. Between 20 and 50 families live in one house, which they all help to build. There are separate rooms for each family along the outside and an open space, like a street, down the centre. The Dayaks live near rivers and they build their longhouses on stilts.

Mosque where people go to pray

Air vent

At Matmata, on the edge of the Sahara Desert, people build their houses below the ground. They dig about 9m down into the soft rock. Several other desert peoples also do this because there are not enough stones or trees with which to build houses. Under the ground they can find water and shelter from sandstorms. It is cooler there too during the hot days.

Tunnel entrance

Tunnel leading to surface

Store room

Well

Oven

There is a central courtyard, open to the sky, which has doorways leading off into the underground rooms. Some of the rooms are for families to live in. Others are stables for their animals and storerooms where they keep grain to last them until the next harvest.

2

Fireplace

This is a store room, living room and bedroom. The stone platform is the family bed, which has a fireplace underneath to heat it in cold weather.

1 Tunnel homes

This is Coober Pedy, a small, hot, dusty town in southern Australia, where the average temperature in summer is 38°C. Most of the people are opal miners.

2

Some miners have made their homes in old mine tunnels. It is so much cooler there that tunnels are now being dug specially for living in.

119

Villages

A village on stilts

School house

Well

splitting a coconut

This isolated village in Malaysia is called a kampong. It is built in a jungle clearing, where it is often very hot and wet. The houses are built on stilts to let the air blow round them and keep them cool and dry. There are no roads or shops and there is no electricity. All the water comes from a well in the middle of the village. There is a village school and also a shelter where the women gather to make baskets.

Village in West Africa

Every day of the week there is a market in one of the villages in the dry lands of West Africa, on the edge of the Sahara Desert.

Vegetable garden

Mud-brick house

Basket of millet

Towers for storing millet

Beer made from millet

Chillis

Millet

The land is so dry in this part of Africa that the people find it difficult to grow enough to eat. Every few years they move to find more fertile land, and their old mud houses crumble and disappear from sight.

Families live in groups of huts, built round yards and surrounded by walls. A village is made up of lots of scattered family groups, each with its farming land round it.

In the rainy season, the women grow ground nuts, chillies and vegetables in gardens near their houses. If they grow more than their families can eat, they sell it at one of the markets.

1 Island village

On the Greek island of Santorini the houses are built close together on the hillside above the harbour. The flat land on the island is kept for farming.

In summer it gets very hot and the houses are painted white to reflect the sunlight. Most houses have two storeys and an outside staircase.

2

After the baker has baked the bread in the morning, villagers who do not have ovens bring their midday meals to be cooked while his oven is still hot.

Mats for shade

Nuts

1 An Indian village

In this Indian village the houses are made of stone and mud and are built around courtyards, where the women spend most of their time. The people here are Hindus. In the Hindu religion every family belongs to a special group called a "caste" which lives in a different section of the village.

2

When the women go to fetch water from the well, they also do their washing. Then they do not have to carry so much water home and can talk while they work.

England

In many English villages the houses face on to a green. There is usually a public house where people can meet, and a village church. People used to live and work in villages but now most of them travel to towns to work.

Cities

1 Cities round the world

Edinburgh, the capital of Scotland, grew up round a huge rock and castle where the people thought they would be safe from attack.

Eighty years ago Nairobi, in Kenya, was a village. When the railway was built, the city grew round it. Now giraffes in the Game Park can see modern blocks.

In the centre of New York are some of the highest skyscrapers in the world. The city began as a landing place for the first European settlers of America.

Living in cities

Some cities have grown over many centuries from villages or small towns. Others have grown up in just a few years. There is always a reason for a city to be where it is. People may have settled there because it was an easy place to defend from enemies, because it was a good centre for trade, or because it had the things needed for an industry.

In many cities, people live close together in old houses and flats. There are no gardens for children to play in.

On the edge of cities, richer people live in houses with gardens. They have to travel into the city centres to work.

There are not enough cheap houses in many cities. Poor people build shanty towns round them, using wood, tin or mud.

So many people have moved into some cities, such as Calcutta in India, that there are no houses for them. They sleep in the streets.

Factories provide jobs for people but they may put smoke and dirt into the air. Travelling to them can be crowded and unpleasant.

Shop windows filled with radios, televisions and furniture bring visitors to cities. Some may stay, hoping to find work.

In cities there are hospitals and doctors. People come in from the countryside where there may be no doctors to care for them.

Sydney, on the coast of Australia, was founded where inlets made a natural, safe harbour. This is now crossed by ferries and a huge bridge.

Cairo stands on the River Nile in Egypt, near the ancient pyramids of Giza. It is Africa's most crowded city. Every day more people come, looking for jobs.

Rio de Janeiro lies beneath Sugar Loaf Mountain on the coast of Brazil. It has fine houses on the beaches but shanty towns have been put up on the hillsides nearby.

New York street

Parks in cities are pleasant places for people to walk and for children to play. The trees give shade for people to sit in and help to improve the air in smoky cities.

Adventure playgrounds have been built in some city centres, often on unused land. Here children can play and have fun, safe from the traffic on the roads.

During the hot summers in New York and other cities, many people sit, talk and play in the streets. It is cooler there than in their small flats and houses. The streets are closed to traffic on some special holidays and parties are held on the pavements and in the roads.

Sports centres, stadiums and swimming pools are built in cities. Here, large numbers of people can watch and learn many sports.

123

Special places to live

Living on an oil rig

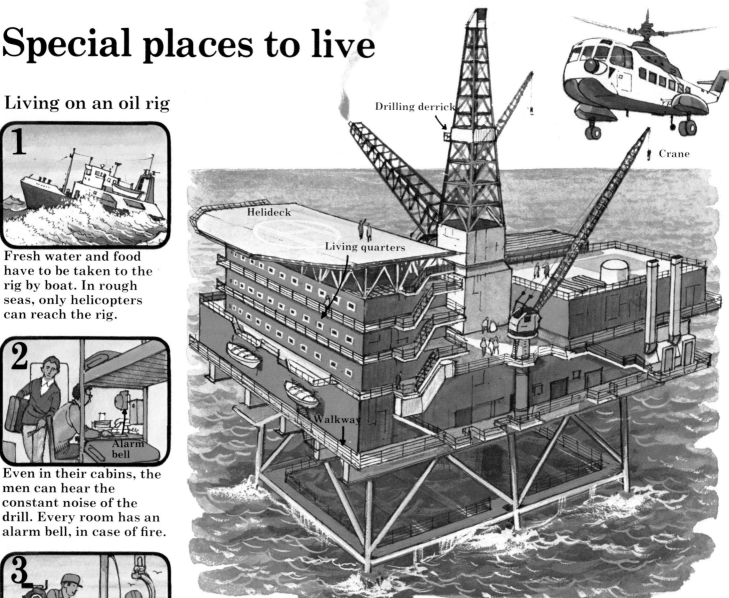

1 Fresh water and food have to be taken to the rig by boat. In rough seas, only helicopters can reach the rig.

2 Even in their cabins, the men can hear the constant noise of the drill. Every room has an alarm bell, in case of fire.

Alarm bell

3 Workers on the drilling platform are called roughnecks. There is always someone working as the drill never stops.

Drilling derrick

Crane

Helideck

Living quarters

Walkway

Tanks filled with water.

Oil rigs are built on shore and towed out to sea. The legs are filled with water to make them sink.

About 90 men live and work on this oil rig. They spend seven days on the rig, working 12 hour shifts and then fly ashore by helicopter for a week's leave.

The oil rig has to be securely anchored to the sea bed so that it does not break loose in rough seas. Divers regularly check the massive anchors which hold it in place.

Dome house

Domes, like this, have been built by people experimenting with new kinds of houses. They even used old car bodies.

1 Zome house

This "Zome" house is heated by the sun. The walls are made of a special material which keeps heat in.

2 Drums filled with water

One wall of the zome is lined with drums filled with water. The sun heats the water and the hot water heats the house.

Lighthouse

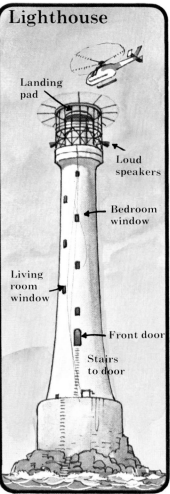

Landing pad

Loud speakers

Bedroom window

Living room window

Front door

Stairs to door

All the rooms in a lighthouse are round and the beds are curved to fit the walls. These have to be very thick to withstand the pounding of the waves. Three men live here, looking after the light and foghorn. Helicopters land on the landing pad on the top even in rough weather.

Under the sea

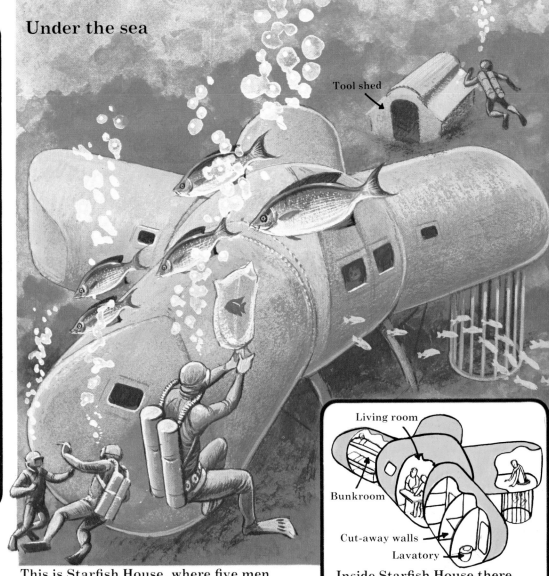

Tool shed

This is Starfish House, where five men lived for a month, studying fish and plants. It was anchored to the sea floor, 10m under the Red Sea, and made of very strong steel so that it could bear the weight of the water. Air was pumped inside the house, but the men wore breathing apparatus when they swam out into the sea.

Living room

Bunkroom

Cut-away walls

Lavatory

Inside Starfish House there were bunkrooms, a living room, kitchen, bathroom and laboratory. Round the door was a cage where the divers could swim when they saw sharks.

Space city

Space ship from Earth docking into space city.

In the future, people may live in cities in space, rather than on the crowded Earth. This vast space city would spin round so that it would feel like being on Earth.

Giant mirrors would reflect sunlight into the city and energy from the sun would be used for power and heat. Special screens would protect it from harmful rays.

Inside space city

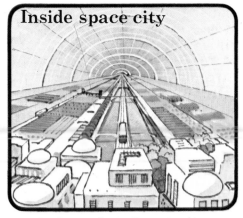

Inside the spokes of space city there would be houses, factories and farmland. There would be air inside the city so people could breathe normally.

Building materials

Stone

Stone makes strong, fire-proof, long-lasting buildings, though it is heavy to lift and transport. Mortar, a mixture of sand, cement* and water, is usually used to hold the stones together. Stones stacked up without mortar make "dry" stone walls.

Quarry where stone is cut from the ground.

House built of roughly cut stones held together with mortar.

"Dry" stone domed roofs on houses in southern Italy.

Concrete

Concrete is a modern building material made of gravel (tiny stones), sand and cement. Mixed with water, it makes a stiff paste which sets hard in hours. When steel rods are added, it is called reinforced concrete and is extremely strong.

Concrete, brought ready-mixed in a tanker, is piped into moulds.

Ready-made concrete walls are lifted into place by giant cranes.

Bricks

When clay is baked at high temperatures, it becomes very hard. It is used for making building bricks, roof tiles and pipes. Different coloured bricks are made from clays found in different places.

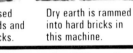

Brick factory where clay is moulded and baked into bricks.

Bricklayers always use mortar to hold bricks in place.

Mud

Mud is plentiful, cheap and easy to work with. It is often mixed with chopped straw to give it extra strength. Some soils bake rock-hard in the sun and may last for hundreds of years, though mud houses need regular repairs.

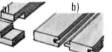

Mud paste is pressed into wooden moulds and left to dry into bricks.

Dry earth is rammed into hard bricks in this machine.

Houses made of mud bricks held together with mud paste.

Wood

Wood rots easily in damp weather and must be given regular coats of paint or varnish to protect it. It also catches fire easily. In forested places, it is a cheap building material. It is widely used for making roof frames.

Tree trunks are cut into planks at saw mills.

Two ways of joining wood: a) a corner joint, b) planks side-by-side.

House built with smoothed planks of wood in southern U.S.A.

Small house in Canada built of whole logs, joined with nails.

Bamboo, grass and leaves

Bamboo plants grow quickly in hot, wet countries and their stems make a strong and flexible, but very light, building material. Grass, reeds and leaves are light and waterproof too, though when dry they easily catch fire.

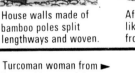

House walls made of bamboo poles split lengthways and woven.

African house woven like a giant basket from split bamboo.

House made of tall reeds by Marsh Arab people in Iraq.

Lakeside house in Peru made of reeds sewn into mats.

Wool and skins

People who move around with their herds of animals need light, portable homes. They often make them from animal skins or hair, supported by branches or wooden poles. Unwashed wool contains natural oils which make it waterproof.

◄ Turcoman woman from Iran making tent felt from sheep's wool. The wool is beaten with sticks and rolled so its fibres tangle together into thick felt.

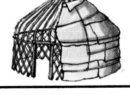

◄ The pieces of felt are stretched over a wooden frame to make a large tent called a yurt. Smoke turns the white felts black after a few years.

Building to suit the climate

Here are some of the ways people make their houses suit the climate they live in.

◄ Thick walls keep the heat out in summer and the cold out in winter.

Houses with windows facing a courtyard keep cool and shady.

▼ Pale colours reflect the sun's rays so walls do not absorb their heat.

◄ Shutters made of slats of wood (louvres) let in cool breezes, but keep out the sun's glare.

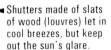

Wooden shutters protect windows from strong winds and snow-storms.

Windscoops direct wind down into houses in this hot Pakistani town.

*Cement is made from a rock called limestone. It sets very hard when mixed with water.

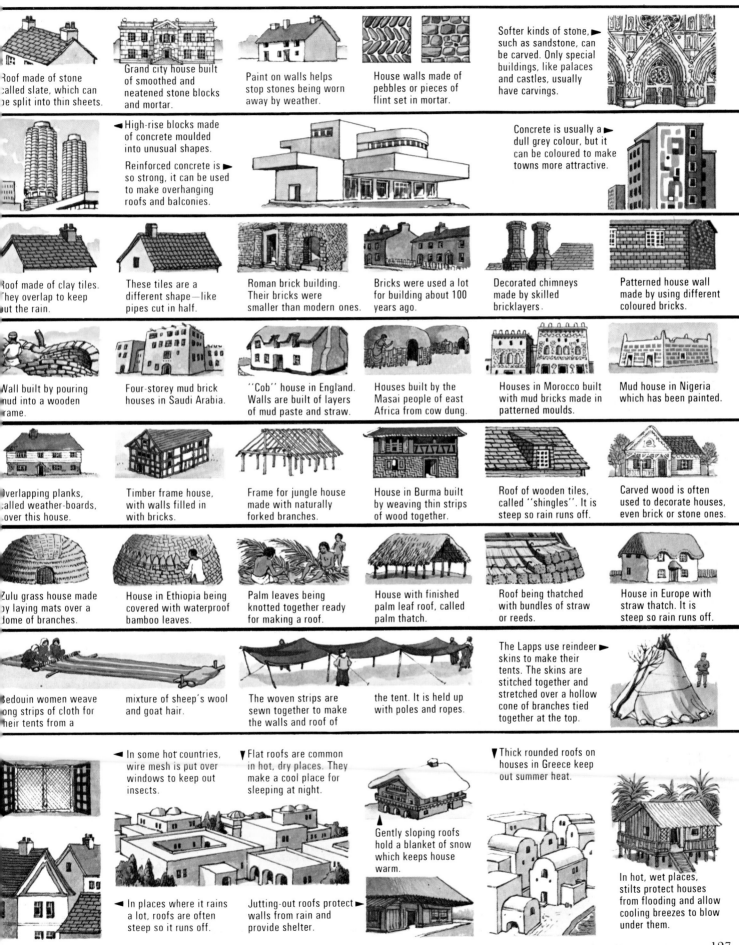

Roof made of stone called slate, which can be split into thin sheets.

Grand city house built of smoothed and neatened stone blocks and mortar.

Paint on walls helps stop stones being worn away by weather.

House walls made of pebbles or pieces of flint set in mortar.

Softer kinds of stone, such as sandstone, can be carved. Only special buildings, like palaces and castles, usually have carvings.

◄ High-rise blocks made of concrete moulded into unusual shapes.

Reinforced concrete is ► so strong, it can be used to make overhanging roofs and balconies.

Concrete is usually a ► dull grey colour, but it can be coloured to make towns more attractive.

Roof made of clay tiles. They overlap to keep out the rain.

These tiles are a different shape—like pipes cut in half.

Roman brick building. Their bricks were smaller than modern ones.

Bricks were used a lot for building about 100 years ago.

Decorated chimneys made by skilled bricklayers.

Patterned house wall made by using different coloured bricks.

Wall built by pouring mud into a wooden frame.

Four-storey mud brick houses in Saudi Arabia.

"Cob" house in England. Walls are built of layers of mud paste and straw.

Houses built by the Masai people of east Africa from cow dung.

Houses in Morocco built with mud bricks made in patterned moulds.

Mud house in Nigeria which has been painted.

Overlapping planks, called weather-boards, cover this house.

Timber frame house, with walls filled in with bricks.

Frame for jungle house made with naturally forked branches.

House in Burma built by weaving thin strips of wood together.

Roof of wooden tiles, called "shingles". It is steep so rain runs off.

Carved wood is often used to decorate houses, even brick or stone ones.

Zulu grass house made by laying mats over a dome of branches.

House in Ethiopia being covered with waterproof bamboo leaves.

Palm leaves being knotted together ready for making a roof.

House with finished palm leaf roof, called palm thatch.

Roof being thatched with bundles of straw or reeds.

House in Europe with straw thatch. It is steep so rain runs off.

Bedouin women weave long strips of cloth for their tents from a

mixture of sheep's wool and goat hair.

The woven strips are sewn together to make the walls and roof of

the tent. It is held up with poles and ropes.

The Lapps use reindeer ► skins to make their tents. The skins are stitched together and stretched over a hollow cone of branches tied together at the top.

◄ In some hot countries, wire mesh is put over windows to keep out insects.

▼ Flat roofs are common in hot, dry places. They make a cool place for sleeping at night.

▼ Thick rounded roofs on houses in Greece keep out summer heat.

Gently sloping roofs hold a blanket of snow which keeps house warm.

◄ In places where it rains a lot, roofs are often steep so it runs off.

Jutting-out roofs protect ► walls from rain and provide shelter.

In hot, wet places, stilts protect houses from flooding and allow cooling breezes to blow under them.

127

House words

Here are some words to do with houses and what they mean. Look out for different kinds of roofs, windows and other parts of houses when you are walking or driving around.

Each floor of a building is called a **storey**. One-storey houses, like this one, are sometimes called bungalows.

Tall blocks of flats with several storeys are called **multi-storey** buildings.

This house is **detached**, which means that it is not joined on to any other houses.

A **semi-detached** house is joined to another house on one side only.

Houses joined to other houses on both sides are called **terraced** houses.

Parts of a house

Eaves · Lintel · Cornice

The underneath parts of a roof where it overhangs a wall are called the **eaves**.

A **lintel** is a long piece of stone or wood over a window or door to hold up the wall above.

A strip of plaster or wood between a wall and roof is a **cornice**.

Decorated boards along the edge of a roof are called **bargeboards**.

A room with glass walls and roof, built on to the side of a house is a **conservatory**.

A **balcony** is a platform built on the outside of an upper floor of a building.

A triangular-shaped end wall of a building is called **gable end**.

Jetty

The beams which support an overhanging upper floor make a **jetty**.

Large stones which strengthen and protect the corners of buildings are called **cornerstones**.

Pediment

A round or triangular-shaped decoration over a window is called a **pediment**.

A platform with a roof but no wall, round the outside of a house is a **verandah**.

A **patio** is a paved area or courtyard outside a house.

Roofs

A roof with slopes on all sides is called a **hipped roof**.

A roof with two slopes on each side, the lower one steeper than the upper, is a **mansard roof**.

A **castellated roof** has battlements to make it look like an old castle.

This curly shape at the edge of a roof is called a **Dutch gable**.

A roof with slopes on all sides, with some slopes shorter than others, is a **half-hipped roof**.

A roof which slopes on two opposite sides only is called a **gabled roof**.

The step shapes at the end of this gabled roof are called **crow-steps** or **corbie-steps**.

Many modern buildings have **flat roofs** of reinforced concrete.

Two gabled roofs side-by-side on a building make an "**M**"-shaped gable.

Windows and doors

Windows that open outwards on hinges are **casement windows**.

A three-sided window in a wall jutting out from a building is a **bay window**.

A **dormer window** is a small window sticking out from a sloping roof.

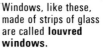

A tall arched window with a shorter, flat-topped window on each side is a **Venetian window**.

Windows, like these, made of strips of glass are called **louvred windows**.

A door which opens in two halves, like this, is called a **stable door**.

Windows with frames that slide up and down are called **sash windows**.

A window which juts out from an upper floor is an **oriel window**.

   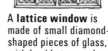

Long windows which reach to the floor and are used as doors are called **French windows**.

A **lattice window** is made of small diamond-shaped pieces of glass, with lead between them.

A semi-circular or fan-shaped window over a door is called a **fanlight**.

A flat window in a roof is called a **skylight**.

Part Five
Maps of the World

Tundra and ice: flat, frozen land with mosses and lichens, but no trees. Long cold winters and short summers.

Mountain vegetation: small, hardy plants and shrubs. Some grass and bare rock. Very high parts covered in snow.

Tropical forest: tall, green, closely growing trees and plants. Thick undergrowth. Very hot and wet.

Cool forest: cool damp forests of coniferous trees. Often snowy in winter.

Desert: very dry, sandy or stony, with very few plats or animals.

Grassland: long grass, bushes and small scattered trees. Hot wet summers and dry winters.

Semi-desert: dry, stoney ground with short grass and low thorny bushes.

Mixed forest and meadow: deciduous and coniferous trees. Mild climate. Rainy all year round.

Mediterranean-type regions: shrubs and trees, mostly evergreens and olives. Warm rainy winters, very dry summers.

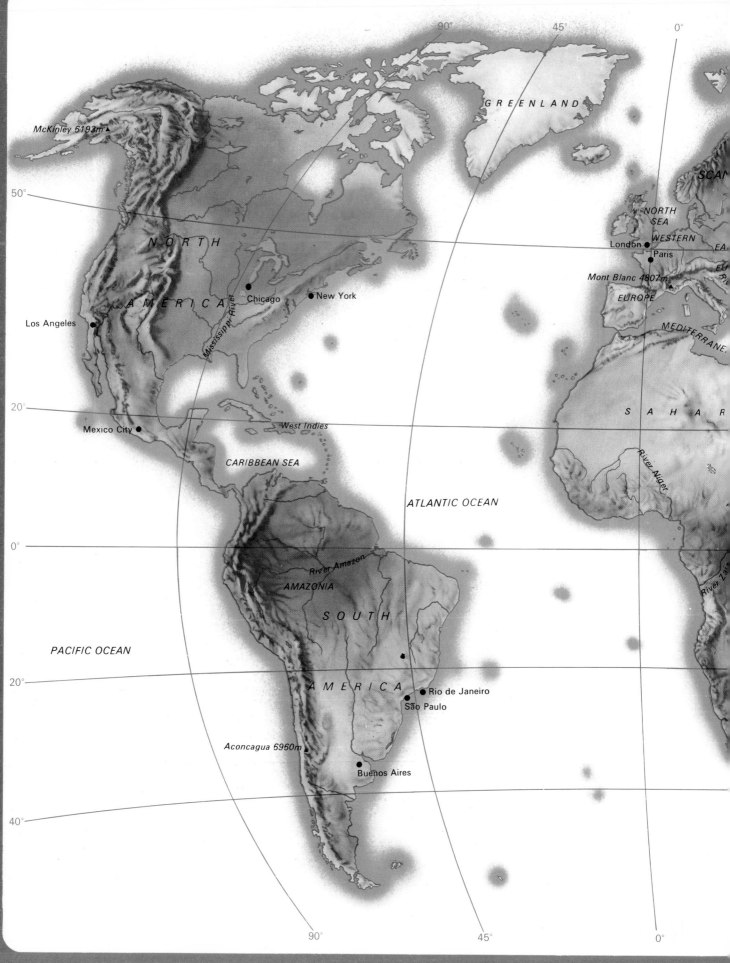

McKinley 5193m▲

GREENLAND

NORTH

50°

NORTH SEA

London ● WESTERN

● Paris

Mont Blanc 4807m▲

EUROPE

SCAN

A M E R I C A

Chicago ●   ● New York

Mississippi River

Los Angeles ●

MEDITERRANE

20°

SAHAR

Mexico City ●

West Indies

River Niger

CARIBBEAN SEA

ATLANTIC OCEAN

0°

River Amazon

AMAZONIA

River Zai

PACIFIC OCEAN

S O U T H

20°

A M E R I C A

● Rio de Janeiro

São Paulo

Aconcagua 6960m▲

Buenos Aires ●

40°

90°   45°   0°

90°   45°   0°

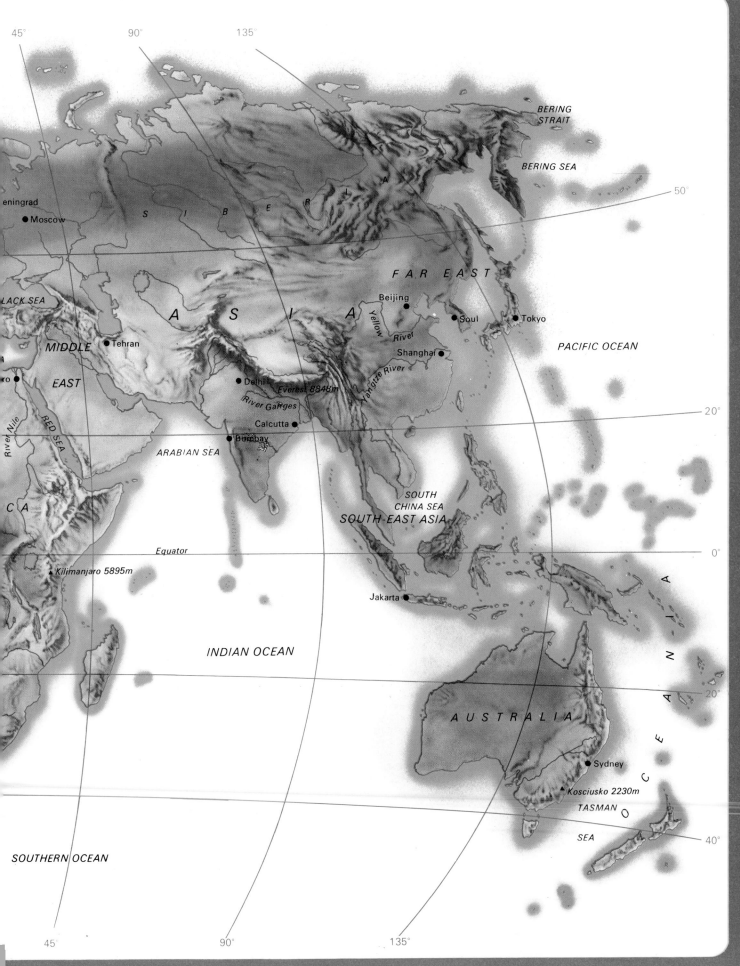

45° 90° 135°

eningrad
● Moscow

S I B E R I A

BERING
STRAIT

BERING SEA

50°

BLACK SEA

A S I A

FAR EAST

Beijing
●

● Soul ● Tokyo

Yellow River

PACIFIC OCEAN

MIDDLE

● Tehran

EAST

● Delhi

Everest 8848m

Shanghai ●

Yangtze River

River Nile

RED SEA

River Ganges

20°

● Calcutta

● Bombay

ARABIAN SEA

CA

SOUTH
CHINA SEA

SOUTH-EAST ASIA

Equator

0°

▲ Kilimanjaro 5895m

Jakarta ●

INDIAN OCEAN

O C E A N I A

20°

A U S T R A L I A

● Sydney

▲ Kosciusko 2230m

TASMAN

SEA

40°

SOUTHERN OCEAN

45° 90° 135°

131

ATLANTIC OCEAN

Natal
Campina Grande
Recife
Maceió
Fortaleza

B R A Z I L

River Tocantins
River São Francisco

Belém

River Xingu
River Tapajos

Cayenne

FRENCH GUIANA

Paramaribo

SURINAME

Georgetown

GUYANA

GUIANA HIGHLANDS

Manaus
River Amazon
River Madeiro

Ciudad Bolivar
River Orinoco

V E N E Z U E L A

Caracas

Barquisimeto
Maracaibo
Lake Maracaibo

River Negro

River Purus

River

C O L O M B I A

Bogota
Medellin
Cali

Buenaventura

Iquitos
River Marañon

A n d e s

Quito

ECUADOR

Guayaquil

Equator

P E R U

Monte Huascaran 5768
Cuzco
Lima
Callao
Trujillo

Georgetown

Kilometres
1000
500
0
Miles
600
300
0

N
E
W
S

SOUTH AMERICA

20°
60°

GUADELOUPE (France)

MARTINIQUE (France)

Dominica
St. Lucia
Barbados
St. Vincent
Grenada

10°

TOBAGO
TRINIDAD
Port of Spain

PUERTO RICO (U.S.A.)
San Juan

Santo Domingo
DOMINICAN REPUBLIC

HAITI
Port-au-Prince

THE BAHAMAS
Nassau

Curacao (Netherlands)

70°

C U B A

Havana

UNITED STATES OF AMERICA

C A R I B B E A N   S E A

80°

Kingston
JAMAICA

Panama Canal
PANAMA
Panamá

GULF OF PANAMA

MEXICO
BELIZE
Belize
GUATEMALA
HONDURAS
Tegucigalpa
EL SALVADOR
San Salvador
NICARAGUA
Managua
COSTA RICA
San José

90°

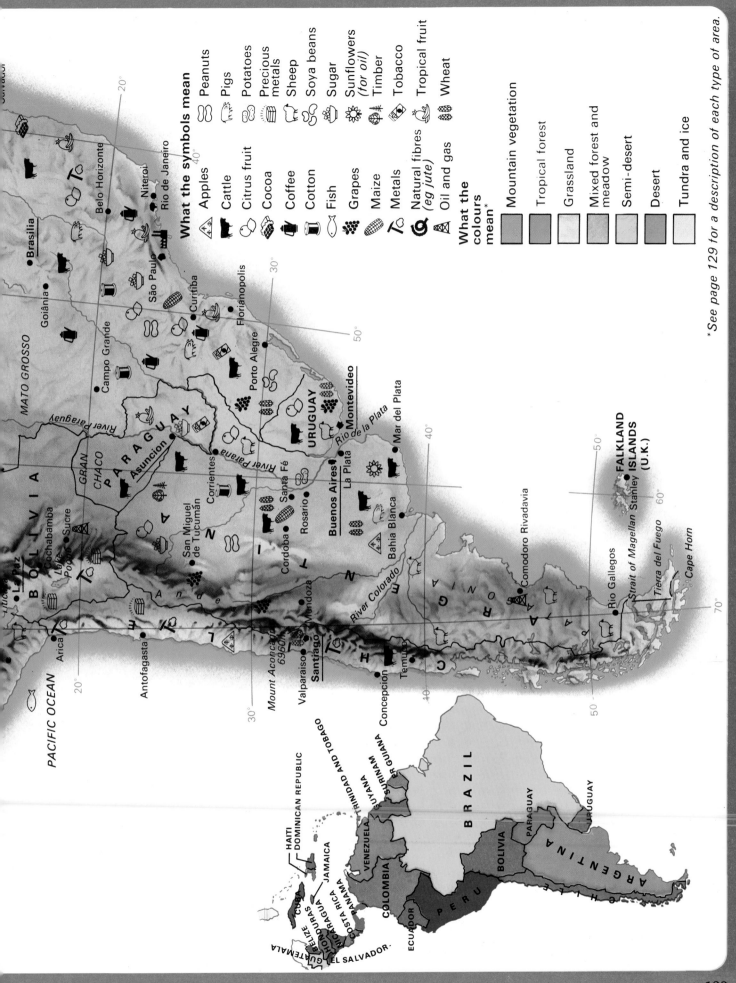

Kilometres

800
500

400
250

0
Miles
0

What the colours mean*

Tundra and ice
Mountain vegetation
Cool forest
Tropical forest
Mixed forest and meadow
Mediterranean-type vegetation
Semi-desert
Desert
Grassland

*See page 129 for a description of each type of area.

N
E
S
W

NORTH AMERICA

U.S.S.R.

BERING STRAIT

70°

180°

160°

River Yukon

Fairbanks

Mount McKinley 5193 m

Alaska Range

Anchorage

GULF OF ALASKA

Arctic circle

Dawson

140°

BEAUFORT SEA

Mackenzie Mountains

River Mackenzie

Great Bear Lake

Yellowknife

Great Slave Lake

Lake Athabasca

120°

100°

80°

Victoria Island

Melville Island

Magnetic North Pole

Baffin   Island

HUDSON STRAIT

Southampton Island

HUDSON BAY

Churchill

Reindeer Lake

60°

Labrador

A

D

A

N

Lake Winnipeg

Lake Manitoba

Saskatoon

Regina

Saskatchewan River

Calgary

Edmonton

A

R O C K Y

C

T

M

Juneau

Queen Charlotte Islands

Vancouver Island

Vancouver

Seattle

50°

Portland

140°

160°

PACIFIC

OCEAN

70°

134

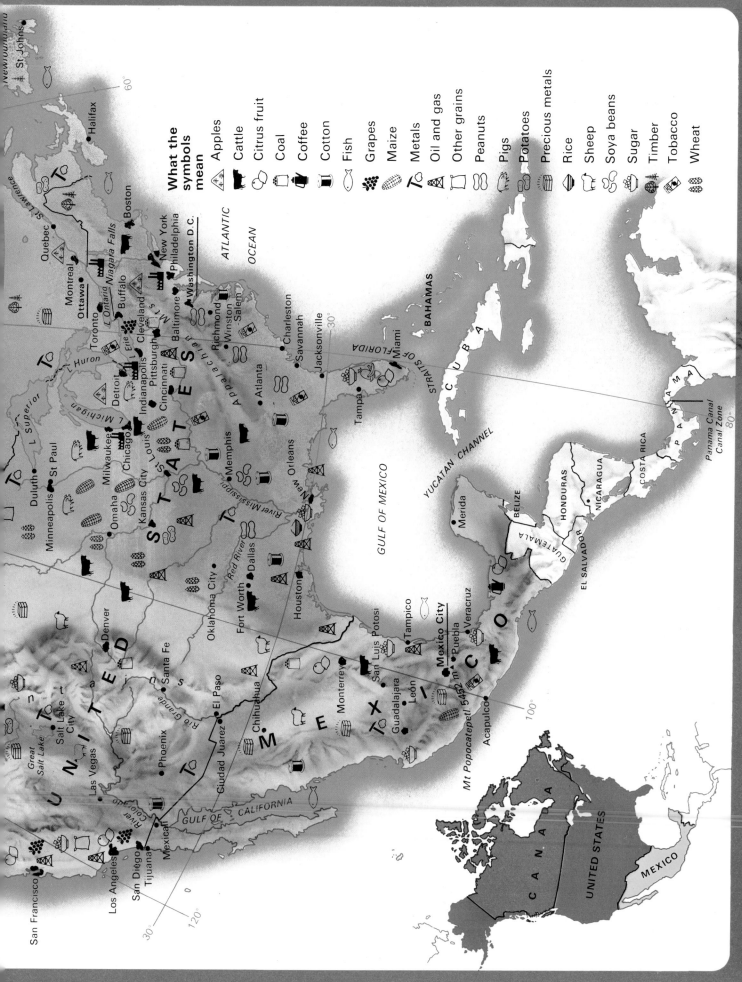

What the symbols mean

- Apples
- Cattle
- Citrus fruit
- Coal
- Coffee
- Cotton
- Fish
- Grapes
- Maize
- Metals
- Oil and gas
- Other grains
- Peanuts
- Pigs
- Potatoes
- Precious metals
- Rice
- Sheep
- Soya beans
- Sugar
- Timber
- Tobacco
- Wheat

St. Johns

Halifax

Quebec
Montreal
Ottawa
Toronto
Buffalo Niagara Falls
Cleveland
Boston
New York
Philadelphia
Washington D.C.
Baltimore
Richmond
Winston Salem

ATLANTIC
OCEAN

L. Ontario
L. Erie
Pittsburgh
Detroit
L. Huron
L. Michigan
Indianapolis
Cincinnati
Charleston
Savannah
Jacksonville

Duluth
St Paul
Minneapolis
Milwaukee
Chicago
St Louis
Memphis
Atlanta

Appalachian Mts

L Superior
UNITED STATES
River Mississippi

Omaha
Kansas City
Tampa

Denver
Oklahoma City
Dallas
Fort Worth
New Orleans

BAHAMAS
STRAITS OF FLORIDA
Miami
CUBA
GULF OF MEXICO

Houston

Santa Fe
El Paso

Salt Lake City
Great Salt Lake
Las Vegas

Phoenix
Rocky Mts
Ciudad Juarez
Rio Grande
Chihuahua
MEXICO

San Francisco
Los Angeles
San Diego
Tijuana
Mexicali
GULF OF CALIFORNIA
River Colorado

Monterrey
San Luis Potosi
Tampico

Guadalajara
León
Mexico City
Puebla
Veracruz
Acapulco
Mt Popocatepetl 5452 m

YUCATAN CHANNEL

Merida
BELIZE
GUATEMALA
HONDURAS
EL SALVADOR
NICARAGUA
COSTA RICA
PANAMA
Panama Canal
Canal Zone

Red River

60°
30°
80°
100°
120°
0°
30°

CANADA
UNITED STATES
MEXICO

Kilometres

0	200	400	
0	150	300	

Miles

What the symbols mean

🔺 Apples
🐄 Cattle
🍋 Citrus fruit
Coal
🐟 Fish
🍇 Grapes
🌽 Maize
Metals
Natural fibres
Oil and gas
Other grains
🐷 Pigs
Potatoes
🐑 Sheep
Sugar
🌻 Sunflowers *(for oil)*
Timber
Tobacco
Wheat

What the colours mean*

Mountain vegetation
Cool forest
Mixed forest and meadow
Mediterranean-type vegetation
Semi-desert

* See page 129 for a description of each type of area.

WESTERN EUROPE

BELGIUM
NETHERLANDS

EAST GERMANY
AUSTRIA
WEST GERMANY
UNITED KINGDOM
IRELAND
FRANCE
SWITZERLAND
ITALY
SPAIN
PORTUGAL

1 LUXEMBOURG
2 LIECHTENSTEIN

POLAND

EAST
WEST

DENMARK
Rostock
Hamburg
River Elbe
Bremen
THE NETHERLANDS
Amsterdam

NORTH SEA

Shetland Islands
Orkney Islands
Aberdeen
Edinburgh
Glasgow
Newcastle
Teesside
Leeds
Sheffield
Manchester
Liverpool
Birmingham
UNITED KINGDOM

Hebrides

Belfast
IRELAND
Dublin
Cork

10°
55°
0°
10°
55°

ATLANTIC OCEAN

ENGLISH CHANNEL

BAY OF BISCAY

CZECHOSLOVAKIA

HUNGARY

YUGOSLAVIA

GERMANY

Leipzig
Dresden
Karl-Marx Stadt
Düsseldorf
Cologne
Bonn
Frankfurt
Nuremberg
Saarbrucken
Stuttgart
Strasbourg
Nancy
Reims

BELGIUM
Brussels
Liège
Lille
Lens
Le Havre
Rouen
Paris
Seine
River Seine
Brest
Channel Islands
Le Mans
Nantes

FRANCE

Dijon
Lyon
River Loire
Clermont-Ferrand
Central Massif
Limoges
Bordeaux
River Dordogne
River Garonne
Toulouse
Nîmes
Pamplona
Pyrenees Mountains
Pico de la Maladeta 3404m
ANDORRA
River Ebro
Saragossa

AUSTRIA
Vienna
Graz
Linz
River Danube
Munich
Salzburg
Innsbruck
Grossglockner S 3798m

SWITZERLAND
Basel
Zurich
Berne
Lake Constance
Jura Mountains
Lake Geneva
Geneva
Grenoble
A Matterhorn
Mont Blanc 4807m
Milan
Turin
Genoa
River Po
Bologna
Florence
Pisa
Elba

Nice
Marseilles
MONACO

SAN MARINO

ITALY
Appennine Mountains
Rome
VATICAN CITY
Naples
Bari

ADRIATIC SEA

Trieste
Venice

Corsica
Ajaccio

Sardinia
Cagliari

Messina
Palermo
Catania
Sicily
Gozo
Malta

Strait of Gibraltar

MEDITERRANEAN SEA

AFRICA

SPAIN
Bilbao
Valladolid
Madrid
River Tagus
Córdoba
Seville
River Guadalquivir
Sierra Nevada
Málaga
Gibraltar (U.K.)
Valencia
Murcia
Alicante
Cartagena
Barcelona
Balearic Islands
Minorca
Majorca
Ibiza

PORTUGAL
Oporto
Lisbon
La Coruña

N
E
S
W

50°
45°
45°
40°
10°
0°
10°

137

EASTERN EUROPE

N
E
S
W

U.S.S.R.

Iaşi
River Siret
Carpathian Mountai

Bialystok
Lublin
P O L A N D
Warsaw
Satu Mare
Cluj
Radom
Kosice
Miskolc
Debrecen
Oradea
Arad
Czestochowa
Cracow
C Z E C H O S L O V A K I A
Budapest
Szeged
Subotica
Lódź
Zabrze Katowice
Gliwice
Kecskemét
River Tisza
Torun
River Wisła
H U N G A R Y
Gdynia
Gdańsk
Ostrava
Bratislava
Györ
Pécs
Bydgoszcz
Poznan
Brno
Lake Balaton
B A L T I C   S E A
River Odra
Wrocław
AUSTRIA
Szczecin
Sudety Mountains
Prague
Zagreb
Ljubljana
E A S T   G E R M A N Y
Rijeka
Istra
Plzen
ITALY
WEST
GERMANY

POLAND
CZECHOSLOVAKIA
HUNGARY
ROMANIA
BULGARIA
YUGOSLAVIA
ALBANIA
GREECE

50°
25°
20°
15°
50°
45°

138

BLACK SEA

Galati
Braila
Bucharest
Ploiesti
Ruse
Danube
River
Craiova
Constanta
Varna
Burgas
Balkan Mountains
BULGARIA
Sofia
Musala 2925m
Plovdiv
Rodopi Mountains
Skopje
TURKEY (in Europe)
Istanbul
Bosporus
SEA OF MARMARA
Gelibolu (Gallipoli)
Dardanelles
TURKEY
Rhodes
Lesbos
Chios
Samos
Mykonos
Naxos
AEGEAN SEA
Thessaloniki
Mount Olympus 2911m
Vólos
Euboea
GREECE
Pindus Mountains
Athens
Piraeus
Patrai
Korinthos
Kalamai
Kithira
Iráklion
Crete

YUGOSLAVIA
Belgrade
Sarajevo
Titograd
Skhodër
Tiranë
ALBANIA
Corfu
IONIAN SEA
Split
Brač
Zadar
Dubrovnik
Dinaric Mountains
ADRIATIC SEA

MEDITERRANEAN SEA

45°
40°
25°
20°
15°

Kilometres
0   100   160   320
0   100   200
Miles

What the symbols mean

⛰ Apples
🐂 Cattle
🍋 Citrus fruit
Coal
🍇 Grapes
Maize
Metals
Natural fibres
Oil and gas
🐖 Pigs
Potatoes
Precious metals
Sheep
Sugar
🌻 Sunflowers *(for oil)*
Tobacco
Wheat

What the colours mean*

Mountain vegetation
Cool forest
Mixed forest and meadow
Semi-desert
Mediterranean-type vegetation

See page 129 for a description of each type of area.

139

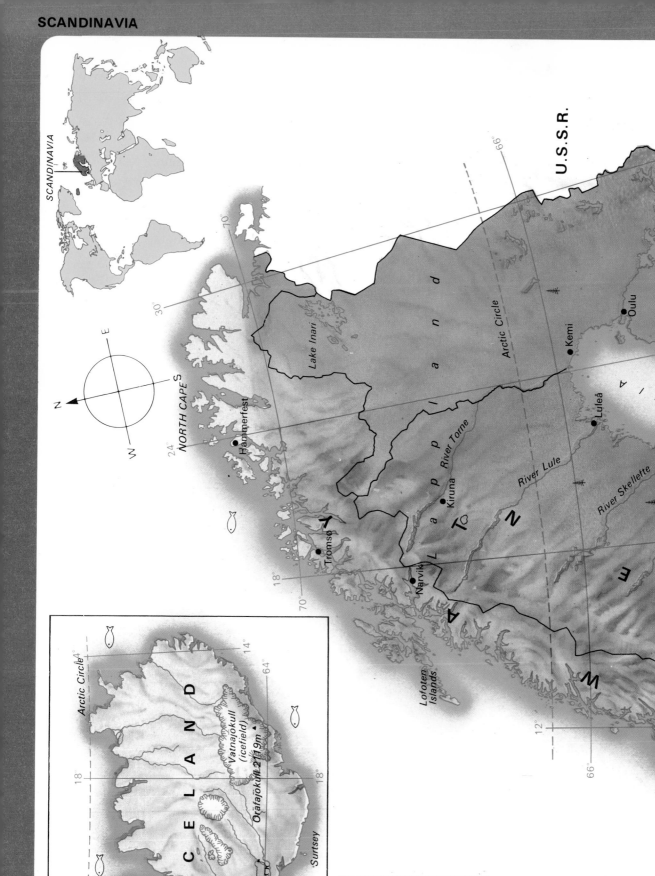

SCANDINAVIA

U.S.S.R.

70°

30°

NORTH CAPE

Hammerfest

N
E
W
S

24°

18°

70°

Tromsø

Narvik

Lofoten
Islands

Lake Inari

L   a   p   p   l   a   n   d

River Torne

Kiruna

River Lule

River Skellette

River Ume

Luleå

Umeå

Kemi

Oulu

Arctic Circle

66°

B   O   T   H   N   I   A

L   A   P   L   A   N   D

S   W   E   D   E   N

M

N   O   R

12°

66°

Trondheim fjo

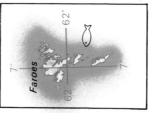

Arctic Circle

64°

14°

64°

18°

18°

22°

22°

22°

64°

I   C   E   L   A   N   D

Vatnajökull
(icefield)

Öræfajökull 2119m ▲

Surtsey

Reykjavik

62°

7°

7°

62°

62°

Faroes

140

What the symbols mean

- Cattle
- Fish
- Metals
- Other grains
- Pigs
- Potatoes
- Sugar
- Timber
- Wheat

What the colours mean*

- Tundra and ice
- Mountain vegetation
- Cool forest
- Mixed forest and meadow

See page 129 for a description of each type of area.

Kilometres
0   100   150   300

Miles
0   100   200

ICELAND

NORWAY

SWEDEN

FINLAND

DENMARK

Helsinki
Lahti
Tampere
Turku
Åland Islands
Åland
GULF

Sundsvall
Uppsala
Stockholm
Västerås
Örebro
Karlstad
Norrköping
Linköping
Jönköping
Lake Vänern
Lake Vättern
Lake Mälaren
Göteborg
Gotland
Öland
B   A   L   T   I   C   S   E   A

Oslo
Drammen
Bergen
Stavanger
Kristiansand
Sognefjorden
Hardanger fjord
Jotunheim Mountains
Galdhöpiggen 2469m
Oslofjord
SKAGERRAK

KATTEGAT

DENMARK
Ålborg
Randers
Jutland
Århus
Esbjerg
Odense
Fyn
Sjælland
Copenhagen
Malmö
Bornholm (Denmark)
Nyköbing
Falster
Lolland

WEST
GERMANY

141

W N

S E

BALTIC SEA

FINLAND

BARENTS SEA

Murmansk

WHITE SEA

Novaya Zemlya

KARA SEA

Kaliningrad

Riga

Tallinn

POLAND

Vilnius

Leningrad

Lake Ladoga

Novgorod

Lake Onega

Archangel

River Pechora

Vorkuta

Brest

Minsk

Lvov

ROMANIA

Gomel

Kiev

Kalinin

Yaroslavl

Moscow

Komsomolsk

Ivanovo

Bryansk

Tula

Ryazan

Gor'kiy

Kirov

River Don

Kishinev

River Dnieper

Kursk

Kharkov

Voronezh

Kazan

Izhevsk

Perm

Nizhny Tagil

River Ob

SI

Odessa

Kherson

Krivoi Rog

Zaporozhe

Dnepropetrovsk

Donetsk

Penza

Togliatti

River Kama

Sverdlovsk

Sevastopol

Yalta

BLACK SEA

Voroshilovgrad

Rostov on Don

Saratov

Kuibyshev

Ufa

Tyumen

Krasnodar

Volgograd

River Volga

Orenburg

Chelyabinsk

Magnitogorsk

Batumi

Grozny

Caucasus Mountains

Astrakhan

CASPIAN SEA

TURKEY

Tbilisi

Yerevan

UNION OF SOVIET SOC

Omsk

Novosibirsk

Tomsk

Kemerovo

Novokuzne

Baku

Barnaul

Semipalatinsk

Krasnovodsk

ARAL SEA

Karaganda

Lake Balkhash

Ashkhabad

IRAN

River Amu

Tashkent

Alma Ata

CHINA

Samarkand

Frunze

Dushanbe

Tien Shan Mountains

AFGHANISTAN

90°

River Irtysh

Ural Mountains

Kilometres

0   200   400

0   320   640

Miles

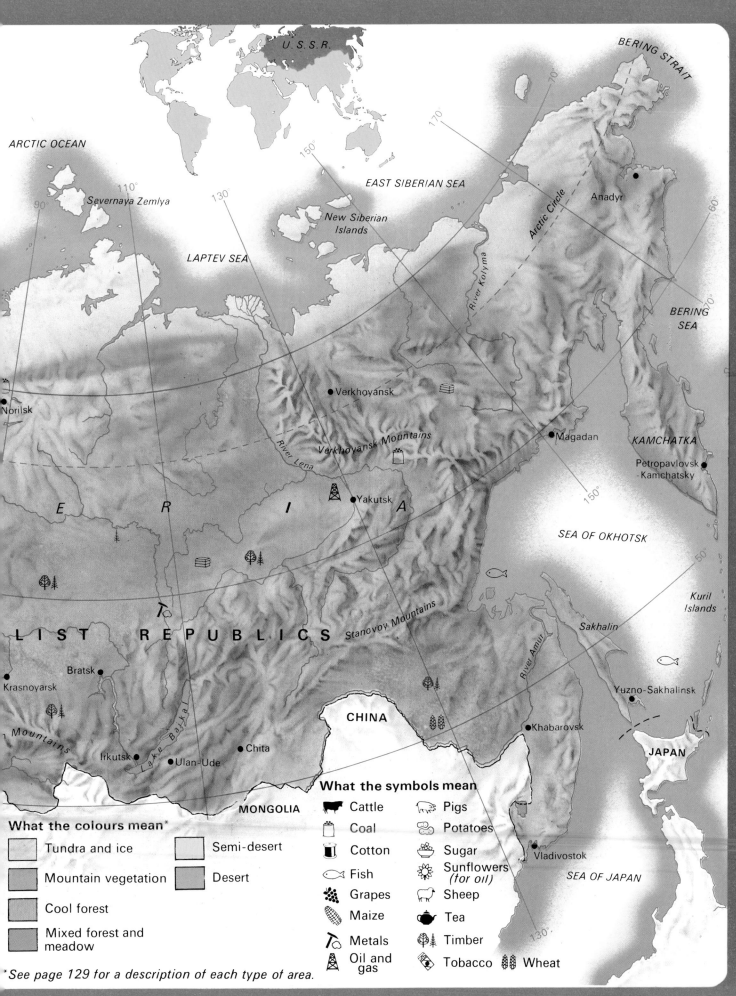

ARCTIC OCEAN

U.S.S.R.

BERING STRAIT

Severnaya Zemlya

90°   110°   130°   150°   170°   70°

EAST SIBERIAN SEA

New Siberian
Islands

LAPTEV SEA

Arctic Circle   Anadyr   60°

River Kolyma

BERING
SEA

Norilsk

Verkhoyansk

E   R   I   A

Magadan

KAMCHATKA

Verkhoyansk Mountains

River Lena

Petropavlovsk
-Kamchatsky

Yakutsk   150°

SEA OF OKHOTSK

50°

Kuril
Islands

L I S T   R E P U B L I C S   Stanovoy Mountains   Sakhalin

River Amur

Bratsk

Krasnoyarsk   Yuzno-Sakhalinsk

CHINA

Khabarovsk

Mountains   JAPAN

Irkutsk   Lake Baikal   Chita

Ulan-Ude   Vladivostok

MONGOLIA   SEA OF JAPAN

What the symbols mean

🐄	Cattle	🐖	Pigs
	Coal		Potatoes
	Cotton		Sugar
🐟	Fish		Sunflowers (for oil)
	Grapes	🐑	Sheep
🌽	Maize	🫖	Tea
	Metals		Timber
	Oil and gas		Tobacco Wheat

What the colours mean*

Tundra and ice	Semi-desert
Mountain vegetation	Desert
Cool forest	
Mixed forest and meadow	

*See page 129 for a description of each type of area.

143

PAKISTAN

AFGHANISTAN

Meshed

I R A N

Bándar Abbas

Desert of Kevir

Mount Damavand
5671m

Elburz Mountains

Tehran

CASPIAN SEA

Isfahan

Shiráz

Dubai

Hamadán

Kermanshah

Zagros Mountains

Ahwaz

Abadan

PERSIAN GULF

Doha

BAHRAIN

Al Manamah

U.S.S.R.

Tabriz

Lake Urmiyeh

Kuwait City

KUWAIT

Basra

Kirkuk

Mount Ararat
5165m

Erzurum

Lake Van

Mosul

River Tigris

Baghdad

I R A Q

Kurdistan

M e s o p o t a m i a

S A U D I

T U R K E Y

BLACK SEA

Samsun

River Kizil Irmak

Ankara

Kayseri

Adana

Aleppo

River Euphrates

SYRIA

Damascus

Syrian Desert
(Badiet esh sham)

Istanbul

Bursa

Konya

Izmir

Antalya

CYPRUS Nicosia

Beirut

LEBANON

Haifa

Tel Aviv

ISRAEL

Gaza

Jerusalem

Amman

JORDAN

Dead Sea

Palestine

Sinai

MEDITERRANEAN SEA

Anatolia

Suez Canal

EGYPT

144

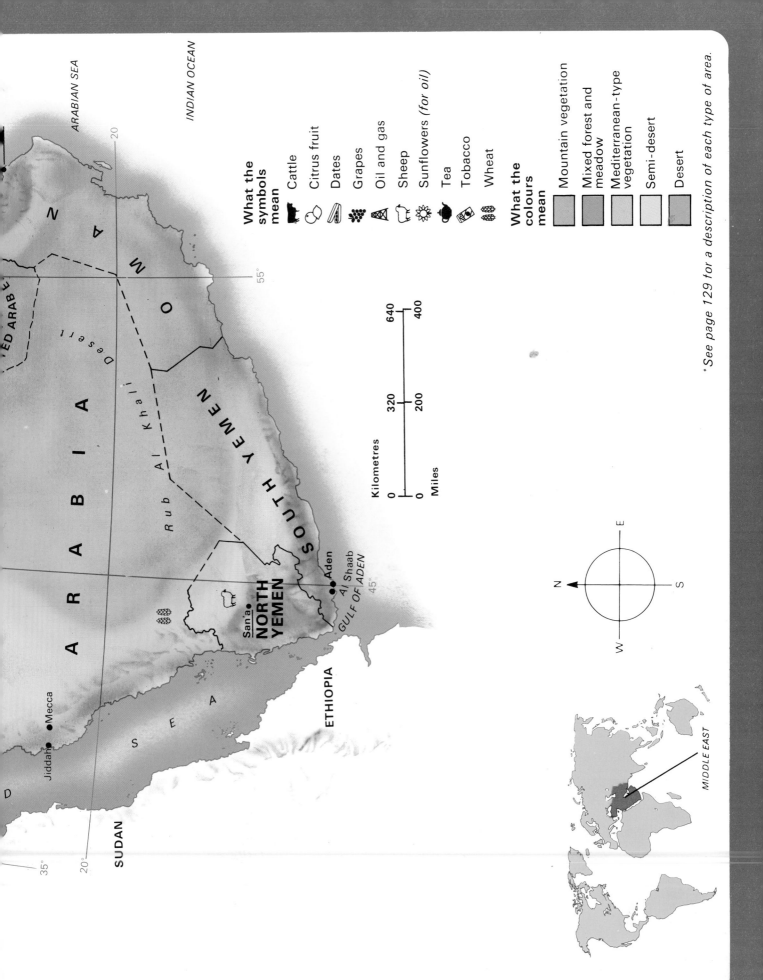

ARABIAN SEA

INDIAN OCEAN

What the symbols mean

- Cattle
- Citrus fruit
- Dates
- Grapes
- Oil and gas
- Sheep
- Sunflowers (*for oil*)
- Tea
- Tobacco
- Wheat

What the colours mean

- Mountain vegetation
- Mixed forest and meadow
- Mediterranean-type vegetation
- Semi-desert
- Desert

*See page 129 for a description of each type of area.

20

55

640

400

320

200

Kilometres

Miles

0

0

UNITED ARAB E

O M A N

Desert

A R A B I A

Rub Al Khali

SOUTH YEMEN

San'a
NORTH
YEMEN

Aden
Al Shaab
GULF OF ADEN

45°

ETHIOPIA

Mecca

Jiddah

D

SUDAN

35°

20°

R   E   D   S   E   A

N
W   E
S

MIDDLE EAST

AFRICA

N
W — E
S

CANARY ISLANDS
(SPAIN)
Las Palmas

Tangier
Rabat
Casablanca
Marrakech
Fès
M O R O C C O
Atlas Mountains
Oran
Algiers
Constantine
Tunis
TUNISIA
Tripoli
Benghazi
L I B Y A
Tibesti
Range
3415m
A h a g g a r
S a h a r a
D e s e r t
A L G E R I A
M A U R I T A N I A
Nouakchott
Dakar
Tombouctou
River Niger
N I G E R
MEDITERRANEAN SEA
SPAIN
ITALY
GREECE
TURKEY
Alexandria
Port Said
Suez Canal
Suez
Cairo
E G Y P T
Lake Nasser
Aswan
River Nile
Omdurman
Port Sudan
RED SEA
SAUDI ARABIA

MOROCCO
TUNISIA
ALGERIA
LIBYA
EGYPT
MAURITANIA
MALI
NIGER
CHAD
SUDAN
ETHIOPIA
DJIBOUTI
SOMALIA
SENEGAL 1
2
GUINEA
SIERRA LEONE
LIBERIA
IVORY COAST
GHANA
TOGO
BENIN
BURKINA FASO
NIGERIA
CAMEROON
CENTRAL
AFRICAN
REPUBLIC
CONGO
GABON 3
4
ZAIRE
UGANDA 5
KENYA
6
TANZANIA
ANGOLA
ZAMBIA
MALAWI
MOZAMBIQUE
ZIMB
ABWE
BOTS
WANA
NAMIBIA
SOUTH AFRICA 7
8
COMOROS
MALAGSY

20°
40°
20°
0°
20°

146

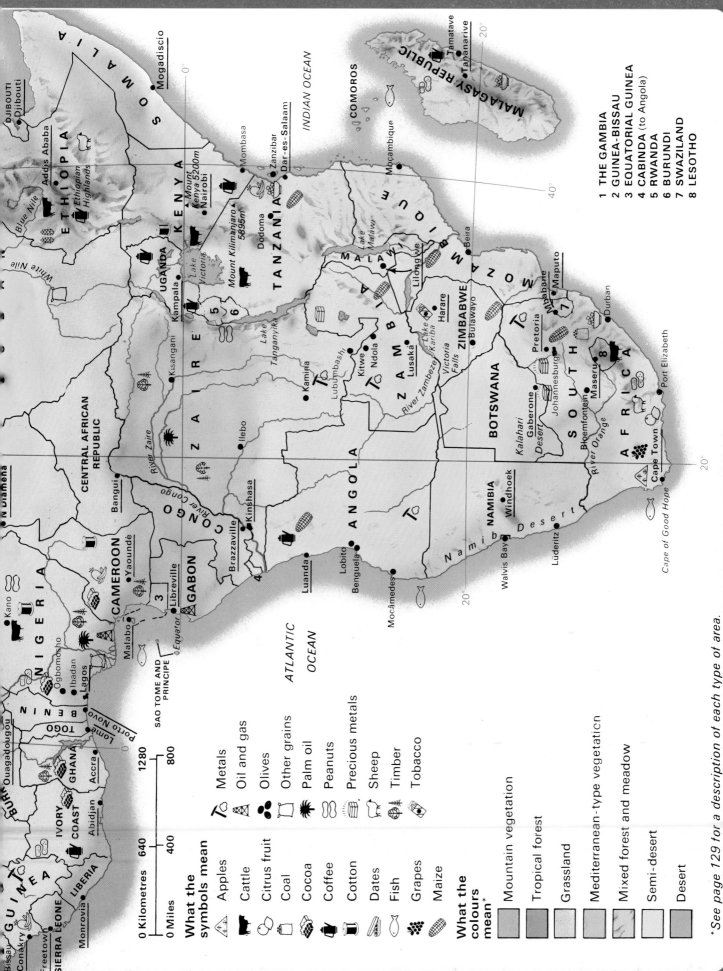

DJIBOUTI
Djibouti
Addis Ababa
ETHIOPIA
Blue Nile
Ethiopian Highlands
White Nile
SOMALIA
Mogadiscio

Mombasa
Mount Kenya 5200m
Nairobi
KENYA
Zanzibar
Dar-es-Salaam
INDIAN OCEAN
COMOROS

Mount Kilimanjaro 5895m
Dodoma
TANZANIA
Lake Victoria
UGANDA
Kampala
Kisangani
ZAIRE

Lake Tanganyika
5
6
Lake Malawi
MALAWI
Lilongwe
Moçambique
MALAGASY REPUBLIC
Tamatave
Tananarive
20°
40°

Beira
MOZAMBIQUE
Harare
ZIMBABWE
Bulawayo
ZAMBIA
Lusaka
Lubumbashi
Kitwe
Ndola
Kamina
River Zambeze
Lake Kariba
Victoria Falls
Ilebo

Mbabane
7
Maputo
Pretoria
Johannesburg
SOUTH AFRICA
Maseru
8
Durban
Port Elizabeth
Bloemfontein
River Orange

BOTSWANA
Kalahari Desert
Gaberone
NAMIBIA
Windhoek
Namib Desert
Walvis Bay
Lüderitz
ANGOLA
Luanda
Lobito
Benguela
Moçâmedes
Cape Town
Cape of Good Hope
20°

N'Djamena
CENTRAL AFRICAN REPUBLIC
Bangui
CONGO
Brazzaville
Kinshasa
River Zaire
River Congo
4
CAMEROON
Yaoundé
3
Libreville
GABON
Malabo
SAO TOME AND PRINCIPE
Equator
ATLANTIC OCEAN
20°

GUINEA
Bissau
Conakry
SIERRA LEONE
Freetown
LIBERIA
Monrovia
IVORY COAST
Abidjan
GHANA
Accra
Kano
NIGERIA
Ogbomosho
Ibadan
Lagos
BENIN
TOGO
Lomé
Porto Novo
BURKINA
Ouagadougou

1 THE GAMBIA
2 GUINEA-BISSAU
3 EQUATORIAL GUINEA
4 CABINDA (to Angola)
5 RWANDA
6 BURUNDI
7 SWAZILAND
8 LESOTHO

0 Kilometres   640   1280
0 Miles   400   800

What the symbols mean

Apples
Cattle
Citrus fruit
Coal
Cocoa
Coffee
Cotton
Dates
Fish
Grapes
Maize
Metals
Oil and gas
Olives
Other grains
Palm oil
Peanuts
Precious metals
Sheep
Timber
Tobacco

What the colours mean*

Mountain vegetation
Tropical forest
Grassland
Mediterranean-type vegetation
Mixed forest and meadow
Semi-desert
Desert

* See page 129 for a description of each type of area.

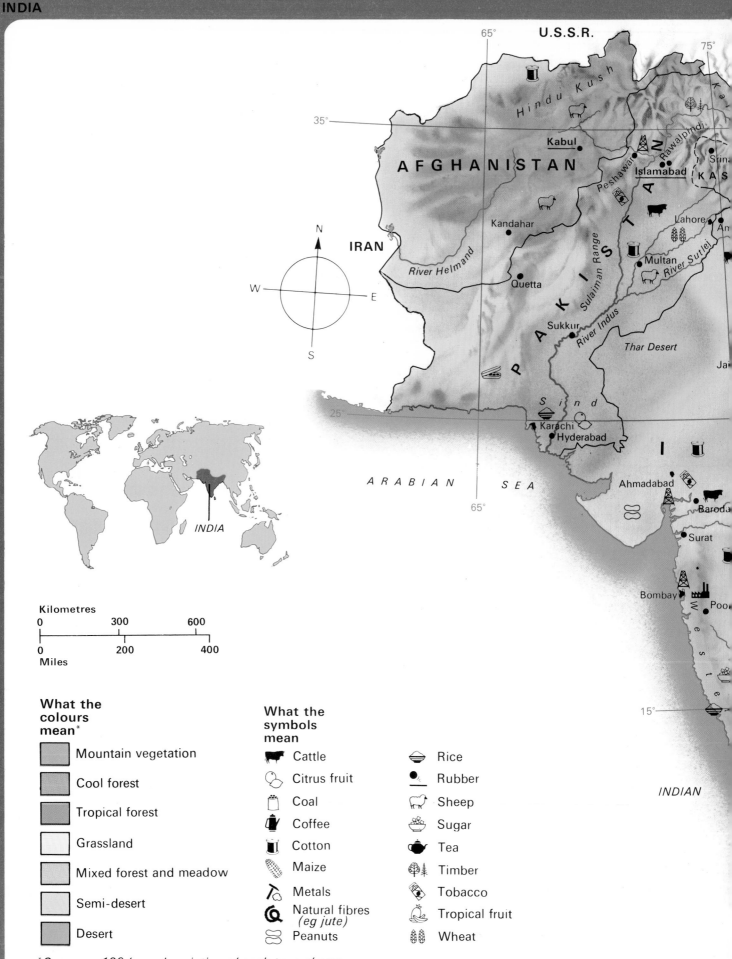

What the colours mean*

- Mountain vegetation
- Cool forest
- Tropical forest
- Grassland
- Mixed forest and meadow
- Semi-desert
- Desert

What the symbols mean

- Cattle
- Citrus fruit
- Coal
- Coffee
- Cotton
- Maize
- Metals
- Natural fibres *(eg jute)*
- Peanuts
- Rice
- Rubber
- Sheep
- Sugar
- Tea
- Timber
- Tobacco
- Tropical fruit
- Wheat

*See page 129 for a description of each type of area.

Kilometres
0   300   600

0   200   400
Miles

35°

CHINA

95°

NEPAL

Mount Everest (8848m)

Delhi
Bareilly

Thimbu
BHUTAN

Katmandu

Darjeeling

River Brahmaputra

25°

Agra

Kanpur
Lucknow

Patna

Varanasi

Sylhet

Imphal

River Jamuna

River Ganges

Allahabad

BANGLADESH
Dacca

BURMA

I N D I A

Bhopal

Jabalpur

Jamshedpur

Howrah
Calcutta

95°

Chittagong

ore

River Narmada

Nagpur

Cuttack

BAY OF

BENGAL

River Godavari

c c a n

ishna

Sholapur

Warangal

Hyderabad

Vishakhapatnam

15°

Eastern

Madras

Ghats

Bangalore

Mysore

OCEAN

River

Cauvery

PALK STRAIT

chin

Madurai

Trivandrum

Trincomalee

SRI
LANKA

Colombo

Kandy

AFGHANISTAN

PAKISTAN

NEPAL

BHUTAN

I N D I A

BANGLADESH

SRI LANKA

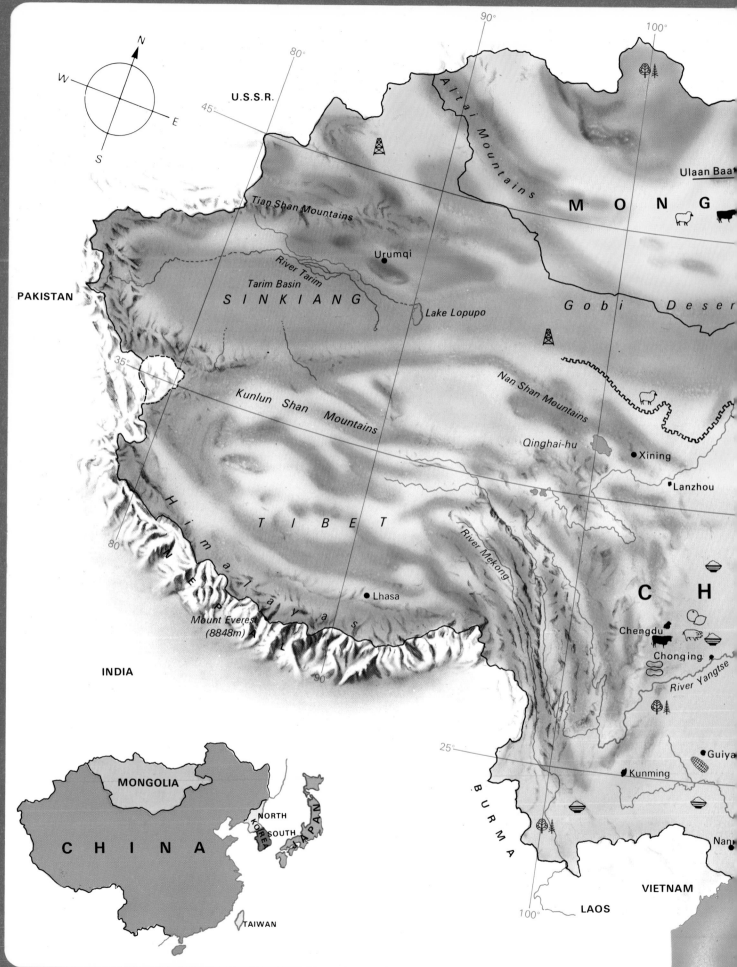

N
W   E
S

U.S.S.R.

Altai Mountains

M O N G

Ulaan Baa

Tian Shan Mountains

Urumqi

River Tarim

Tarim Basin

Gobi   Deser

S I N K I A N G

Lake Lopupo

PAKISTAN

Nan Shan Mountains

Kunlun Shan Mountains

Qinghai-hu

Xining

Lanzhou

T I B E T

River Mekong

C   H

H i m a l a y a s

Lhasa

Mount Everest
(8848m)

Chengdu

INDIA

Chonging

River Yangtse

Guiya

Kunming

MONGOLIA

B U R M A

NORTH
KOREA
SOUTH

C H I N A

JAPAN

Nan

TAIWAN

VIETNAM

LAOS

45°

80°

90°

100°

35°

80°

90°

25°

100°

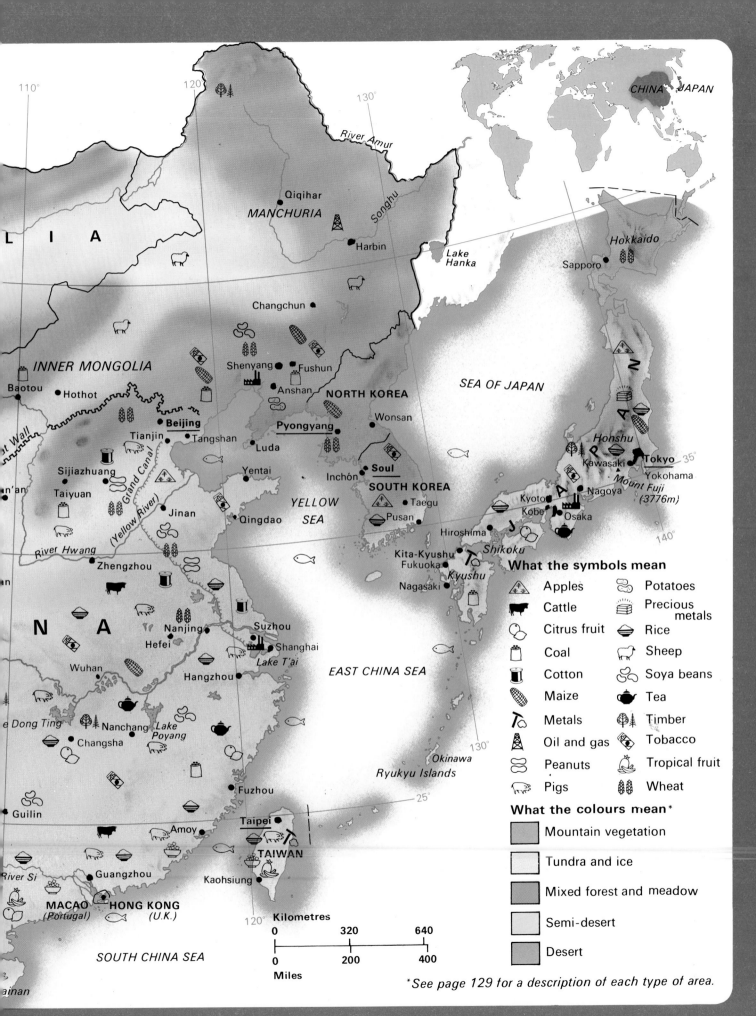

110°

120°

130°

River Amur

Qiqihar

MANCHURIA

Songhu

Harbin

Lake Hanka

CHINA   JAPAN

Hokkaido

Sapporo

Changchun

INNER MONGOLIA

SEA OF JAPAN

Shenyang   Fushun

Baotou

Hothot

Anshan

NORTH KOREA

Wonsan

ot Wall

Tianjin

Beijing

Tangshan

Pyongyang

Luda

Honshu

Kawasaki   Tokyo   35

Sijiazhuang

Yentai

Soul

Yokohama

n'an

Taiyuan

Grand Canal

Inchón

SOUTH KOREA

Mount Fuji
(3776m)

Jinan

Qingdao

YELLOW
SEA

Taegu

Kyoto

Nagoya

140°

Kobe

Osaka

(Yellow River)

Pusan

River Hwang

Hiroshima

J

Zhengzhou

Kita-Kyushu

Shikoku

What the symbols mean

N   A

Fukuoka

Kyushu

Apples   Potatoes

Nanjing

Suzhou

Nagasaki

Cattle   Precious
                metals

Hefei

Shanghai

Citrus fruit   Rice

Wuhan

Hangzhou

Lake T'ai

EAST CHINA SEA

Coal   Sheep

Cotton   Soya beans

e Dong Ting

Nanchang

Lake
Poyang

Maize   Tea

Changsha

Metals   Timber

Okinawa

Oil and gas   Tobacco

Ryukyu Islands

Fuzhou

25

Peanuts   Tropical fruit

Guilin

Pigs   Wheat

Amoy

Taipei

What the colours mean*

TAIWAN

Mountain vegetation

River Si

Guangzhou

Kaohsiung

120

Tundra and ice

MACAO
(Portugal)

HONG KONG
(U.K.)

Mixed forest and meadow

Kilometres

Semi-desert

0   320   640

Desert

SOUTH CHINA SEA

0   200   400

Miles

*See page 129 for a description of each type of area.

ainan

151

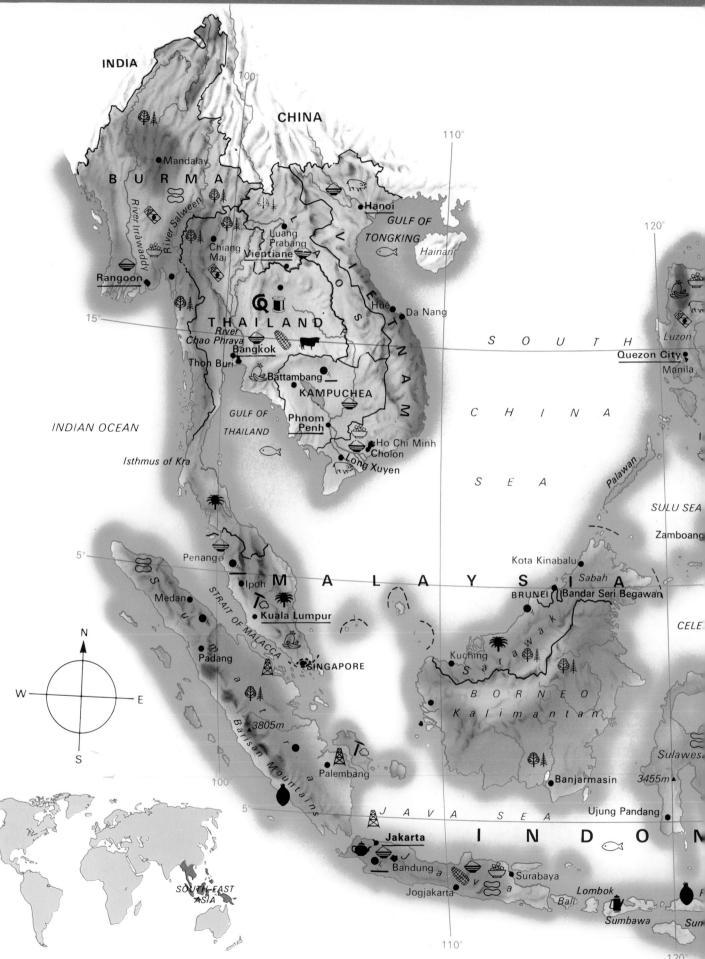

INDIA

CHINA

Mandalay

B U R M A

River Salween

River Irrawaddy

Chiang
Mai

Luang
Prabang

Vientiane

L A O S

Hanoi

GULF OF
TONGKING

Hainan

100°

110°

120°

Rangoon

15°

Hué

Da Nang

T H A I L A N D

River
Chao Phraya

V I E T N A M

S O U T H

Bangkok

Thon Buri

Battambang

KAMPUCHEA

GULF OF
THAILAND

Phnom
Penh

Ho Chi Minh
Cholon

Long Xuyen

C H I N A

Quezon City

Manila

Luzon

INDIAN OCEAN

Isthmus of Kra

S E A

SULU SEA

Zamboanga

Palawan

5°

Penang

M A L A Y S I A

Kota Kinabalu

Sabah

CELE

Ipoh

BRUNEI

Bandar Seri Begawan

Medan

S
u
m
a
t
r
a

STRAIT OF MALACCA

Kuala Lumpur

Kuching

S a r a w a k

Padang

SINGAPORE

B O R N E O

K a l i m a n t a n

Sulawesi

N

W   E

S

3805m

Banjarmasin

3455m

Barisan Mountains

Palembang

Ujung Pandang

100

5

J A V A   S E A

Jakarta

I N D O N

110°

Bandung

Surabaya

Jogjakarta

Lombok

Bali

Sumbawa

Sum

120°

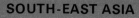

SOUTH-EAST
ASIA

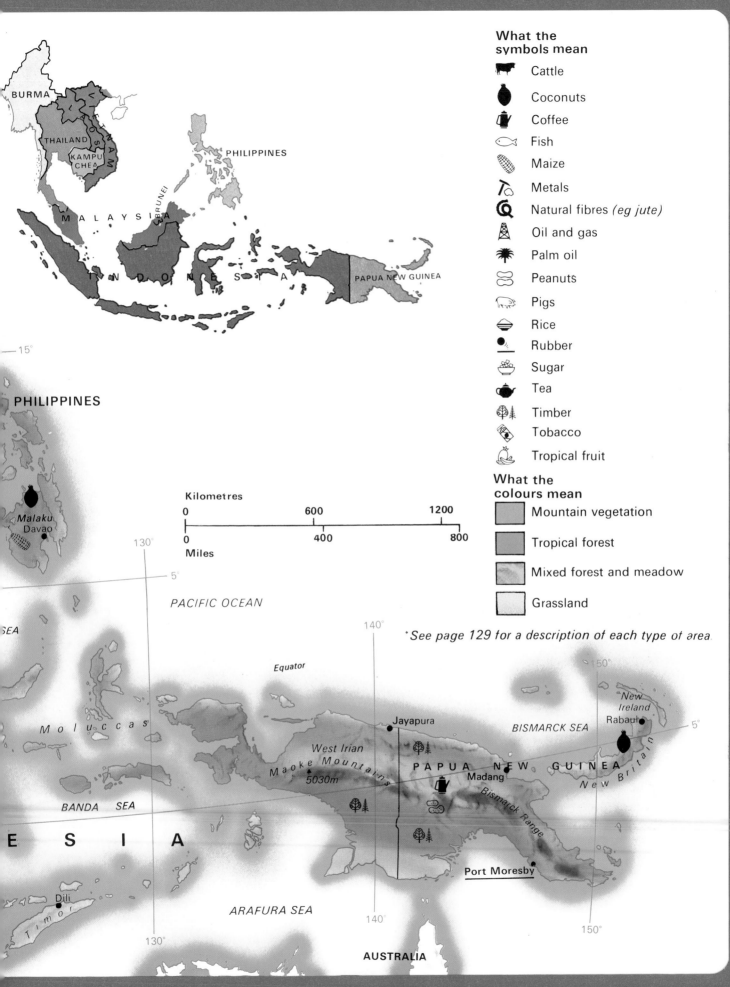

What the symbols mean

- 🐄 Cattle
- Coconuts
- Coffee
- 🐟 Fish
- Maize
- Metals
- Natural fibres *(eg jute)*
- Oil and gas
- Palm oil
- Peanuts
- 🐖 Pigs
- Rice
- Rubber
- Sugar
- Tea
- Timber
- Tobacco
- Tropical fruit

What the colours mean

	Mountain vegetation
	Tropical forest
	Mixed forest and meadow
	Grassland

*See page 129 for a description of each type of area.

BURMA

THAILAND

KAMPU CHEA

VIETNAM

LAOS

MALAYSIA

BRUNEI

PHILIPPINES

INDONESIA

PAPUA NEW GUINEA

PHILIPPINES

Malaku
Davao

Kilometres

0   600   1200

0   400   800

Miles

PACIFIC OCEAN

Equator

Moluccas

Jayapura

BISMARCK SEA

New
Ireland
Rabaul

West Irian

Maoke Mountains
5030m

PAPUA NEW GUINEA

Madang

New Britain

Bismarck Range

BANDA SEA

E S I A

Dili

Timor

ARAFURA SEA

Port Moresby

AUSTRALIA

130°

5°

130°

5°

140°

140°

150°

150°

15°

153

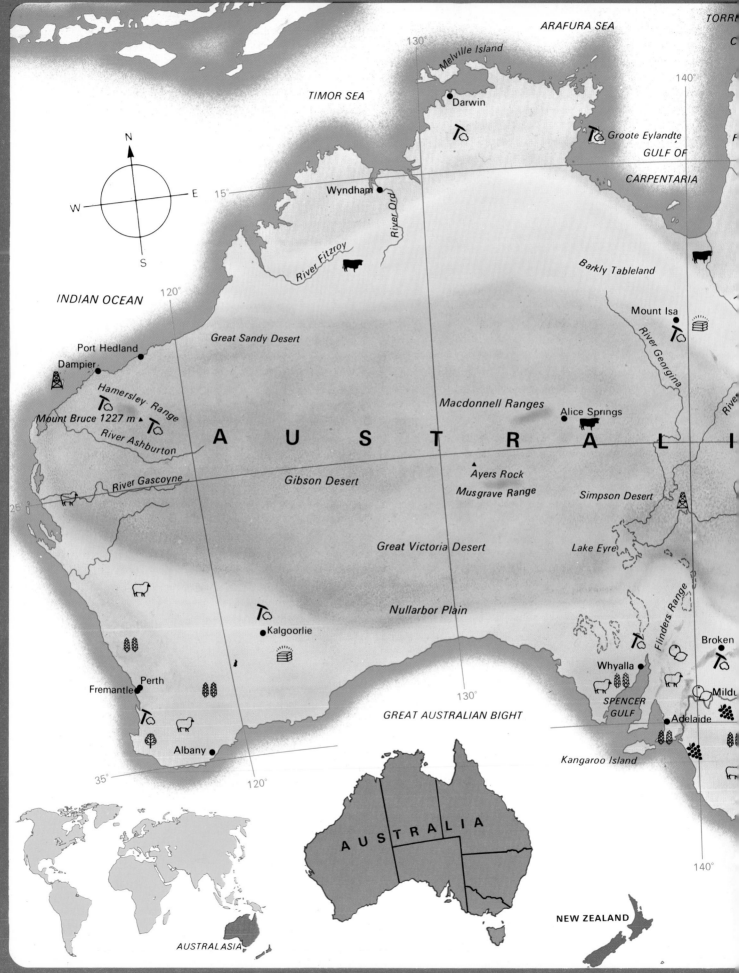

ARAFURA SEA

TORR

TIMOR SEA

130°

140°

Melville Island

Darwin

Groote Eylandte

GULF OF

CARPENTARIA

15°

Wyndham

River Ord

River Fitzroy

Barkly Tableland

INDIAN OCEAN

120°

Great Sandy Desert

Mount Isa

River Georgina

Port Hedland

Dampier

Hamersley Range

Mount Bruce 1227 m ▲

River Ashburton

Macdonnell Ranges

Alice Springs

River

A U S T R A L I

River Gascoyne

Gibson Desert

Ayers Rock

Musgrave Range

Simpson Desert

25°

Great Victoria Desert

Lake Eyre

Nullarbor Plain

Flinders Range

Kalgoorlie

Broken

Whyalla

Perth

Fremantle

SPENCER
GULF

Mildu

130°

GREAT AUSTRALIAN BIGHT

Adelaide

Albany

Kangaroo Island

140°

35°

120°

AUSTRALIA

A U S T R A L I A

NEW ZEALAND

AUSTRALASIA

PAPUA NEW GUINEA

0 — 400 — 800 Kilometres
0 — 250 — 500 Miles

What the symbols mean

Cattle		Precious metals	
Citrus fruit		Sheep	
Coal		Sugar	
Grapes		Timber	
Metals		Tropical fruit	
Oil and gas		Wheat	

What the colours mean*

Mountain vegetation

Tropical forest

Grassland

Mediterranean-type vegetation

Mixed forest and meadow

Semi-desert

Desert

See page 129 for a description of each type of area.

CORAL

SEA

15°

150°

Cairns

Townsville

Mackay

Rockhampton

25°

A

Toowoomba

Darling
Downs

Brisbane

Range

Grafton

Darling

Tamworth

Orange

Newcastle

Blue Mountains

Sydney

Wollongong

ver Murrumbidgee

Canberra

River Murray

Albury

Mount Kosciusko (2230m)

Bendigo

Australian Alps

TASMAN SEA

35°

Melbourne

Geelong

BASS STRAIT

Devonport

150°

Launceston

Tasmania

Hobart

NEW ZEALAND

175°

North Cape

35°

TASMAN SEA

Auckland

North Island

Hamilton

Rotorua

New Plymouth

Lake Taupo

40°

Wanganui

COOK STR

Mount Bruce 1227 m

40°

Nelson

170°

165°

South Island
Franz Josef Glacier
Mount Cook (3764m)

Wellington

35°

Southern Alps

Canterbury Plains

Christchurch

175

45°

MILFORD SOUND

Timaru

Oamaru

45°

Invercargill

Dunedin

Stewart Island

Chatam Islands

170°

50°

165°

155

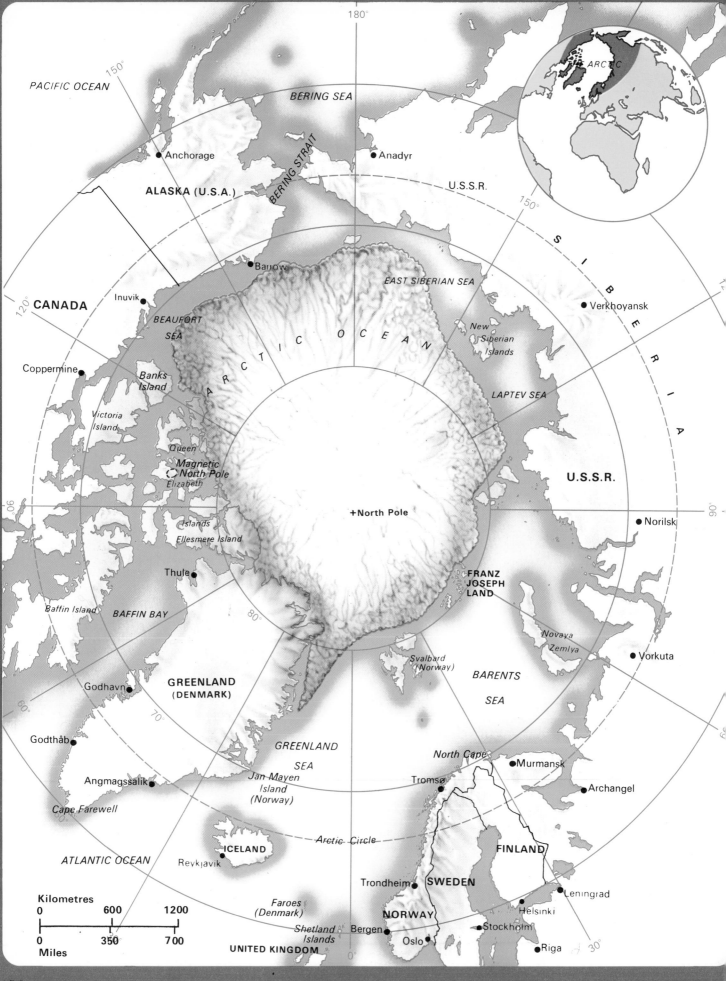

PACIFIC OCEAN

BERING SEA

● Anchorage

● Anadyr

ALASKA (U.S.A.)

BERING STRAIT

U.S.S.R.

150°

180°

150°

S I B E R I A

● Barrow

EAST SIBERIAN SEA

● Verkhoyansk

CANADA

120°

● Inuvik

BEAUFORT
SEA

ARCTIC OCEAN

New
Siberian
Islands

Coppermine ●

Banks
Island

LAPTEV SEA

Victoria
Island

Queen

Magnetic
◯ North Pole

Elizabeth

U.S.S.R.

90°

+North Pole

● Norilsk

90°

Islands
Ellesmere Island

Thule ●

FRANZ
JOSEPH
LAND

Baffin Island

BAFFIN BAY

80°

Novaya
Zemlya

● Vorkuta

Svalbard
(Norway)

BARENTS

Godhavn ●

GREENLAND
(DENMARK)

60°

SEA

70°

Godthåb ●

GREENLAND

North Cape

● Murmansk

Angmagssalik ●

SEA

Tromsø ●

● Archangel

Cape Farewell

Jan Mayen
Island
(Norway)

Arctic Circle

FINLAND

ATLANTIC OCEAN

ICELAND

Reykjavik ●

Trondheim ●

SWEDEN

NORWAY

● Leningrad

Faroes
(Denmark)

Shetland
Islands

UNITED KINGDOM

Bergen ●

Oslo ●

● Helsinki

● Stockholm

● Riga

30°

0°

ARCTIC

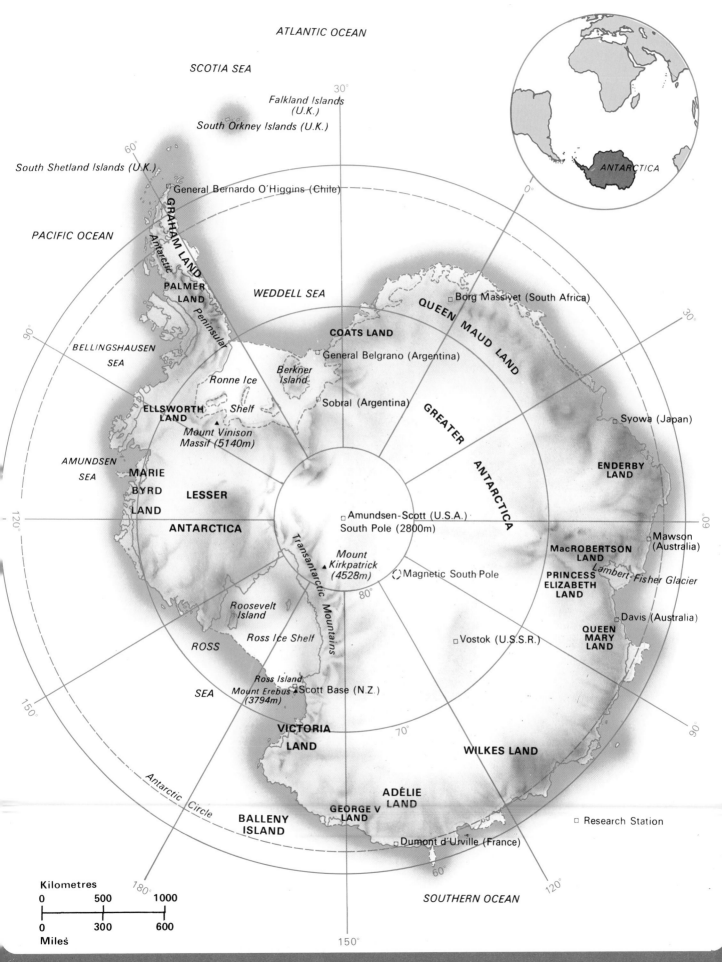

ATLANTIC OCEAN

SCOTIA SEA

Falkland Islands
(U.K.)

South Orkney Islands (U.K.)

South Shetland Islands (U.K.)

General Bernardo O'Higgins (Chile)

PACIFIC OCEAN

30°

60°

90°

GRAHAM LAND

Antarctic

PALMER
LAND

WEDDELL SEA

Peninsular

BELLINGSHAUSEN
SEA

COATS LAND

□ Borg Massivet (South Africa)

QUEEN MAUD LAND

Ronne Ice

Berkner
Island

□ General Belgrano (Argentina)

ELLSWORTH
LAND

Shelf

□ Sobral (Argentina)

GREATER

▲ Mount Vinison
Massif (5140m)

Syowa (Japan)

ANTARCTICA

AMUNDSEN
SEA

MARIE
BYRD
LAND

LESSER

ENDERBY
LAND

ANTARCTICA

□ Amundsen-Scott (U.S.A.)
South Pole (2800m)

Mount
Kirkpatrick
(4528m)

Magnetic South Pole

MacROBERTSON
LAND

Mawson
(Australia)

Lambert-Fisher Glacier

PRINCESS
ELIZABETH
LAND

Transantarctic

□ Davis (Australia)

Roosevelt
Island

QUEEN
MARY
LAND

Ross Ice Shelf

Mountains

□ Vostok (U.S.S.R.)

ROSS

Ross Island
Mount Erebus ▲ Scott Base (N.Z.)
(3794m)

SEA

VICTORIA
LAND

WILKES LAND

ADÉLIE
LAND

Antarctic Circle

GEORGE V
LAND

BALLENY
ISLAND

□ Research Station

□ Dumont d'Urville (France)

SOUTHERN OCEAN

ANTARCTICA

120°

150°

180°

60°

90°

120°

150°

0°

30°

60°

70°

80°

Kilometres

| 0 | 500 | 1000 |

| 0 | 300 | 600 |

Miles

157

Map Index

First published in 1978 by Usborne Publishing Ltd.
20 Garrick Street. London WC2E 9BJ, England.

Copyright © 1978 Usborne Publishing Ltd.
First published in this edition in 1984

The name Usborne and the device ✺ are Trade
Marks of Usborne Publishing Ltd.

Printed in Belgium

General Index